THE GOSPEL
OF THE

HOLY
SPIRIT

Other titles in the Seedbed Daily Text series:

The
Seedbed
Daily Text

THE GOSPEL
OF THE

Mark

J. D. WALT

Printed in the United States of America

Cover and page design by Strange Last Name
Page layout by PerfecType, Nashville, Tennessee

Walt, John David.
   The gospel of the Holy Spirit : Mark / J.D. Walt. – Franklin, Tennessee : Seedbed Publishing, ©2019.

   pages ; cm. – (Seedbed daily text)

   ISBN 9781628247336 (paperback)
   ISBN 9781628247343 (Mobi)
   ISBN 9781628247350 (ePub)
   ISBN 9781628247367 (uPDF)

   1. Bible. Mark -- Meditations. 2. Holy Spirit -- Mediations.
   I. Title. II. Series.

BS2585.54.W34 2019   226.3/06   2019947619

Seedbed

SEEDBED PUBLISHING
Franklin, Tennessee
seedbed.com

Contents

How the Daily Text Works

It seems obvious to say, . . . but the Daily Text is written every day. Mostly, it is written the day before it is scheduled to release online.

Before we go further, I would like to cordially invite you to subscribe and receive the daily e-mail. Visit seedbed.com/dailytext to get started. Also check out the popular Facebook group, Seedbed Daily Text.

Eventually, the daily postings become part of a Daily Text discipleship resource. That's what you hold in your hands now.

It's not exactly a Bible study, though the Bible is both the source and subject. You will learn something about the Bible along the way: its history, context, original languages, and authors. The goal is not educational in nature but transformational. We are more interested in knowing Jesus than knowing *about* Jesus.

To that end, each reading begins with the definitive inspiration of the Holy Spirit, the ongoing, unfolding text of Scripture. Following that is a short and, hopefully, substantive insight from the text and some aspect of its meaning. For insight to lead to deeper influence, we turn the text into prayer. Finally, influence must run its course toward impact.

This is why we ask each other questions. The questions are not designed to elicit information but to crystallize intention.

Discipleship always leads from inspiration to intention and from attention to action.

Using the Daily Text as a Discipleship Curricular Resource for Groups

While Scripture always addresses us personally, it is not written to us individually. The content of Scripture cries out for a community to address. The Daily Text is made for discipleship in community. This resource can work in several different ways. It could be read like a traditional book, a few pages or chapters at a time. Though unadvisable, the readings could be crammed in on the night before the meeting. Keep in mind, the Daily Text is not called the Daily Text for kicks. We believe Scripture is worthy of our most focused and consistent attention. Every day. We all have misses, but let's make every day more than a noble aspiration. Let's make it our covenant with one another.

For Use with Bands

In our judgment, the best and highest use of the Daily Text is made through what we call banded discipleship. A disciple-ship band is a same-gender group of three to five people who read together, pray together and meet together to become the love of God for one another and the world. With banded discipleship, the daily readings serve more as a common text for the band and grist for the interpersonal conversation mill between meetings. The band meeting is reserved for the specialized activities of high-bar discipleship.

To learn more about bands and banded discipleship, visit discipleshipbands.com. Be sure to download the free *Discipleship Bands: A Practical Field Guide* or order a supply of the printed booklets online. Also, be sure to explore Discipleship Bands, our native app designed specifically for the practice of banded discipleship, in the Apple store or at Google Play.

For Use with Classes and Small Groups

The Daily Text has also proven to be a helpful discipleship resource for a variety of small groups, from community groups to Sunday school classes. Here are some suggested guidelines for deploying the Daily Text as a resource for a small group or class setting:

I. Hearing the Text

Invite the group to settle into silence for a period of no less than one and no more than five minutes. Ask an appointed person to keep time and to read the biblical text covering the period of days since the last group meeting. Allow at least one minute of silence following the reading of the text.

II. Responding to the Text

Invite anyone from the group to respond to the reading by answering these prompts: What did you hear? What did you see? What did you otherwise sense from the Lord?

III. Sharing Insights and Implications for Discipleship

Moving in an orderly rotation (or free-for-all), invite people to share insights and implications from the week's readings.

What did you find challenging, encouraging, provocative, comforting, invasive, inspiring, corrective, affirming, guiding, or warning? Allow group conversation to proceed at will. Limit to one sharing item per turn, with multiple rounds of discussion.

IV. Shaping Intentions for Prayer

Invite each person in the group to share a single discipleship intention for the week ahead. It is helpful if the intention can also be framed as a question the group can use to check in from the prior week. At each person's turn, he or she is invited to share how their intention went during the previous week. The class or group can open and close their meeting according to their established patterns.

Introduction

It's the shortest Gospel. That's what I was thinking. There I was, a 2L (second-year law student) heading into the summer months as a highly underqualified, bush-league youth pastor in charge of leading a big-league youth ministry. I didn't know what to do to engage those young people, but I knew one thing for certain . . .

It had to start with the Word of God.

In an effort to find the best intersection of youth on summer break and the Word of God, I chose the shortest Gospel, the Gospel of Mark, with all its sixteen glorious chapters, 678 verses, and 11,304 words.

I wasn't trying to lower the bar but to change the game. I wanted to shift the approach from, "I ought to read my Bible every now and then," to "I must dig into the Word of God every day." We needed to shift from external prodding to internal hunger; from oughts and shoulds to musts and now; from ticking a box to winning a game.

And so began the Mark Pizza Challenge.

To win the challenge and be included in the pizza party to end all pizza parties all you had to do was read the Gospel of Mark, one chapter a day, sixteen days in a row. If you missed a day, it meant starting back over with chapter 1. We allowed unlimited restarts and students (and adults) had the entire summer to get it done.

Stories abounded. The students went all in. It wasn't about the pizza as much as it became about completing the challenge and doing it together.

One kid recounted a story of being at camp and forgetting to read, remembering after lights out and before midnight, and getting out their flashlight in their zipped-up sleeping bag and getting it done to keep the streak alive. Another kid invited his whole non-church going family to join the challenge. The whole thing took on epic proportions as momentum built. Some kids wound up reading it a dozen times after the misses and restarts were all tallied.

When together, we would talk about Mark's Jesus stories as though they had happened that very morning. I will forever remember one of the kids citing the fifth chapter of Mark as a warrant to pray for another of our students who needed physical healing. We went for it. And she was miraculously healed! Like those first disciples, we were astonished!

Through this simple, living way of reading together, we became intrigued by the seemingly secret power of Jesus' prayer life. This seamless sort of intimate conversation between he and his Father inspired us to follow. I will always remember the wonderful sight of too many sleeping bags to count stretched across the front of the sanctuary for the spontaneously called all-night prayer meeting inspired by Mark's gospel. This led to the weekly pre-dawn prayer breakfasts that soon began to awaken the high school. As you are imagining by now, the Pizza Celebration Feast transformed into the veritable banqueting table of the kingdom of heaven.

The challenge led us beyond the comfy confines of a more committed daily devotional life. We were actually following Jesus. These teenagers had grown up in a church seized by the inertia of religious motions and machinations and they weren't having it. They wanted the movement. The Word of God was leading them into the world of God-sized possibilities. The Word of God, the Scriptures, led us to the Word of God, Jesus, and Jesus led us to the Spirit of God. And the Spirit of God, through this band of students, began to sow the seeds of awakening into the whole church that continues to grow and bear fruit to this very day.

We see this articulated in the opening verses of Mark's gospel. The Word of God had come to John in the wilderness. "And this was his message: 'After me comes the one more powerful than I, the straps of whose sandals I am not worthy to stoop down and untie. I baptize you with water, but he will baptize you with the Holy Spirit'" (Mark 1:7–8).

It reminds me of a now-famous story told about the late John Wimber, founder of the Vineyard movement. He was an early member of the band, the Righteous Brothers. Along the way he met Jesus, left his former way of life, and began to immerse himself in the Gospel accounts of Jesus' life. Soon after his conversion, he visited a church and after the church service he approached the pastor with this question:

"So, when do we do the stuff?"

"The stuff," said the pastor. "What's the stuff?"

"You know," John replied, "the stuff in the Bible, like healing the sick and casting out demons. The stuff!"

"Oh," replied the pastor. "We don't do the stuff. We believe they did it back in biblical days, but we don't do it today."

With a rather confused look on his face, John could only say: "And I gave up drugs for this?"

The Word of God led us to Jesus and Jesus was leading us to the Holy Spirit and the Holy Spirit was leading us into a life of doing "the stuff."

It's why I have come to think of Mark's gospel as the gospel of the Holy Spirit. Often when Christians want to learn more about the Holy Spirit they turn to a text like the Acts of the Apostles or they dig into texts like 1 Corinthians 12 and 14 and other New Testament teachings. These are all deep wells of rich learning. For some reason, it seems less obvious to study the person and work of Jesus as a direct curriculum on the Spirit-filled life. In the Gospels, we see what it looks like when the Holy Spirit perfectly and completely inhabits, possesses, and empowers a human being in the midst of the fallen, broken world in which we live.

Jesus does some explicit teaching about the Holy Spirit, but far greater is the demonstration of the Spirit we witness through virtually every aspect of his life. We learn about the ways of the Spirit through his patterned paths of seeking out his Father in secret prayer. We learn about the workings of the Spirit in the tender ways he sees and approaches the humble and broken. A disciple of Jesus must become a student of Jesus in every conceivable fashion. Discipleship is not a life of believing and behaving. It is a life of beholding and becoming. As we behold the Son of God, we become the sons and daughters of God. As we are baptized into his death, we are raised into his life. As we are raised into his life, we are filled with his Spirit. As we are filled with his Spirit, we learn to think after his thoughts and to discern his mind to do the stuff of his work.

As we read and meditate through this shortest Gospel, we will ask one of the biggest questions: What might we learn about the person and work of the Holy Spirit through a close examination of the person and work of Jesus of Nazareth, the Messiah? And how might we proceed accordingly?

This is the stuff of great awakenings. Aren't we ready for more than the next Bible study or a cozier quiet time with our morning coffee? Aren't we tired of church as usual? Aren't we more than a little bit weary of going through the religious motions? Aren't we ready for the great movement of the gospel to once again rise up in our day? Aren't we ready to do the stuff of awakening?

As I look back now, some three decades later, on that summer in Mark's gospel, a.k.a. the Mark Pizza Challenge, I see the germinal seeds of everything I have tried to be about ever since. In those days, the kids sowed the seeds of awakening in me. They showed me what was possible when a sleepy local church begins to shake off the shackles of domesticated religion and digs deep into the well of Word and Spirit, taking up the mantle of the apostolic faith of Jesus. And that's why I left everything else to follow Jesus. It's why we launched Seedbed and New Room and the quest to sow for a great awakening. It's why I write the Daily Text each day. And it's why I dedicate this journey through the shortest Gospel to them.

THE GOSPEL
OF THE
HOLY
SPIRIT

The Gospel of the Holy Spirit: The Age of the Spirit

MARK 1:1 | The beginning of the good news about Jesus the Messiah, the Son of God.

Consider This

What can we learn about the person, work, ways, and will of the Holy Spirit through a close examination of the life of Jesus? What can we learn about the Spirit-infused life that we are called to live by studying Jesus, whom we are called to be like? In other words, Jesus teaches us the ways of the Spirit-filled life if we will pay attention. It's one thing to ask, "What would Jesus do?" It's quite another to inquire about how the Holy Spirit perfects holy love in a us.

A fun yet inferior analogy comes from the Star Wars movies. Luke Skywalker learned the ways of "The Force" by studying at the feet of his Jedi Master, Obi-Wan Kenobi. The Holy Spirit, far from some mythical force, is the third person of the Trinity. Jesus doesn't just teach us about the Holy Spirit when he is speaking explicitly about the Spirit. He teaches us about the ways of the Spirit every day of his life. We will see the Spirit on display from the ordinary to the supernatural. Conversely, the Holy Spirit will teach us about Jesus through the Spirit's presence in our lives, right here and now.

Maybe this is something of what makes the gospel the gospel. The gospel is historical, yet it transcends history. Like a window that cannot be closed, the gospel opens up an eternal vista into the mysterious verities of the Trinity. In fact, it's better than that. The Holy Spirit brings us into the inner workings of the gospel by bringing us inside the interpersonal relationships between Father, Son, and Holy Spirit.

The beginning of the good news about Jesus the Messiah, the Son of God.

Think about it. The Holy Spirit revealed the gospel to Mark, who wrote it down. And by the grace of God, the Holy Spirit will reveal this gospel to us in ever-deepening ways.

Our prayer for these days of Pentecost: "Spirit of the living God, fall afresh on me."

Are you ready?

The Prayer

Spirit of the living God, fall afresh on me.

The Questions

- Do you think it is possible to be filled with the Holy Spirit in the same way Jesus was filled with the Holy Spirit during his life on earth? Why or why not?

When Revival Becomes Awakening: The Age of the Spirit

2

MARK 1:2–6 ESV | As it is written in Isaiah the prophet,

"Behold, I send my messenger before your face, who will prepare your way, the voice of one crying in the wilderness: 'Prepare the way of the Lord, make his paths straight,'"

John appeared, baptizing in the wilderness and proclaiming a baptism of repentance for the forgiveness of sins. And all the country of Judea and all Jerusalem were going out to him and were being baptized by him in the river Jordan, confessing their sins. Now John was clothed with camel's hair and wore a leather belt around his waist and ate locusts and wild honey.

Consider This

Isaiah? Yes! The Holy Spirit is weaving a very long, complex, and intricate plotline. It runs all the way from the original creation to the final consummation of the new creation. Think Adam to Abraham, Eve to Elijah, Isaac to Isaiah, Sarah to Solomon, and on we could go. The gospel comes in the way the Holy Spirit has invited us to enter this story through the life, death, resurrection, and ascension of Jesus Christ and made the invitation effective on the day of Pentecost. We must become lifelong students of this story—not as outside observers but as inside players. This is an intergenerational story and this is our chapter. Isaiah? Yes!

The Word of God comes in the wilderness. Ever since the exile from Eden that has been the story. No matter how much we try to dress it up and make ourselves at home, with nice cars and fancy restaurants, and highly edited Facebook lives, underneath it all is a fallen world. It often takes a stripping away of such accoutrements to realize this. Sometimes fasting can help prepare the way for such a realization. The Spirit of God creates the conditions that make for the prerequisite path of holy discontent. No matter how okay things may appear to be, they are not okay. Great awakenings happen when people begin to respond to the Spirit's movement to make a straight path, to do something different, to interrupt the patterns of so-called prosperity.

What is a baptism of repentance? It signals a clean slate, a fresh start, a new beginning. It is a decisive marking of a moment that holds the possibility of a new movement in one's life. To repent means, in the words of my friend Brian Russell, to realign one's life with a bigger story, a better one. It means recalibration and it leads to renewing. For so many, this isn't the repentance that comes before deciding to follow Jesus, but the repentance that comes after such a decision. It's when holy discontent becomes an awareness of our own brokenness and how that has broken others. It happens when we start getting honest with ourselves, with God, and with others. That's what confession means.

The Holy Spirit is not about creating cool environments for crafty religious experiences. The Holy Spirit creates corporate, collective, and even generational movements. Deeply personal? Yes. Profoundly communal? Yes. When enough of God's people reach the threshold of honesty about their holy discontent, movement begins to happen. Historians call it "revival." Look at today's text. Already, only five verses in, people are coming in droves to hear the Word of God in the wilderness. Revival begins not so much with lost sinners as it begins with saved sinners whose salvation has grown cold. True revival, given a wide berth, always holds the possibility of spilling into the broader culture. This is the stuff of awakenings.

The Holy Spirit works through unlikely characters. At times they can be quite unusual. From coats made of camel hair to a little Pentecostal craziness at times—be discerning, but err on the side of making room for John-the-Baptist types. They often play a forerunning role only a person like them would, or even could, play. It may require some of us shedding some of our dignified religious sophistication if we are to play our roles.

The Prayer

Spirit of the living God, fall afresh on me.

The Questions

- Reflect on a way the Holy Spirit has inspired repentance and realignment in your life.
- How might that be happening now?

3 The Secret Way of Holy Spirit–Filled Fasting

MARK 1:7–13 NRSV | He proclaimed, "The one who is more powerful than I is coming after me; I am not worthy to stoop down and untie the thong of his sandals. I have baptized you with water; but he will baptize you with the Holy Spirit."

In those days Jesus came from Nazareth of Galilee and was baptized by John in the Jordan. And just as he was coming up out of the water, he saw the heavens torn apart and the Spirit descending like a dove on him. And a voice came from heaven, "You are my Son, the Beloved; with you I am well pleased."

And the Spirit immediately drove him out into the wilderness. He was in the wilderness forty days, tempted by Satan; and he was with the wild beasts; and the angels waited on him.

Consider This

The Holy Spirit always points to Jesus. In his short sixteen chapters, Mark brings us the core of the core of the gospel. I love the clarity of, "And this was his message:" in the New International Version (v. 7). John said many things, but in the midst of many things I suspect John always said one thing and it was likely pretty much the same thing. This was his message:

"The one who is more powerful than I is coming after me; I am not worthy to stoop down and untie the thong of his

sandals. I have baptized you with water; but he will baptize you with the Holy Spirit."

That Mark could bring it to such clarity says much more about John than it does about Mark. John was focused on the message. We live in an age where a premium is put on being a great communicator of the gospel. The key is not style points for the messenger, but laser-like focus on the message itself. I often say of myself, "I am an average preacher, but I have an incredible message."

Let me switch gears, though, and put the question to you (preacher or not). If I were to spend the next year alongside you, at the end of that time, how would I summarize your message? Could I bring it to a sentence? What would it be?

The Holy Spirit personalizes the Word of God. Consider Jesus' baptism. John baptized him with water, but the Father baptized him with the Holy Spirit. He saw heaven being torn open. He saw the Holy Spirit, the third person of the Trinity, descending on him as though he were a dove landing on Jesus' shoulder. Then the voice: *"You are my Son, the Beloved; with you I am well pleased."*

So often, the baptism of the Holy Spirit gets spoken of in terms of phenomenology. In other words, it's all about heaven being torn open and a demonstrative manifestation of the Spirit. Entire branches of the church believe the definitive and exclusive sign of the baptism of the Holy Spirit must be the phenomenon of speaking in tongues. While I do not want to diminish the gift of tongues as a manifestation of the sign of the Spirit, I do want to inquire as to why there is no reference to Jesus speaking in tongues? Doesn't it make sense that the baptism of the Holy Spirit would be accompanied primarily by the Word of God?

If I'm staying close to the text, here's my observation: the definitive sign of the baptism of the Holy Spirit is the inward perception of these words from the Father spoken as a pure gift, individually over the sons and daughters of God: "You are my son . . . You are my daughter . . . whom I love; with you I am well pleased." When these words move from believed concept to experienced truth (which is far too rare), it's a primary sign of the baptism of the Holy Spirit. The baptism of the Holy Spirit is literally an internal flood of the holy love of God inside of a person. The definitive *demonstration* of the baptism of the Holy Spirit, of course, is the creative expression of the holy love of God flooding into the world. The rest of the gospel will be the unfolding of this awe-inspiring demonstration. You will see as we move along that I am something of a purist in my belief: As it was with Jesus, so it can be with us.

The Holy Spirit deepens faith through fasting. The Holy Spirit sends the baptized ones straight into the heart of the place formerly known as Eden, which has now become the wilderness. Note the textual details pointed out: the presence of angels, the animal kingdom, and Satan. Note also that Jesus fasted. Eden was a place of perpetual feasting. What if fasting in the wilderness of this world is actually the divine way back to feasting in the kingdom of God (a.k.a. Eden)?

The Prayer

Spirit of the living God, fall afresh on me.

The Questions

What if fasting is the divinely appointed means to sustain the fullness of the baptism of the Holy Spirit in the wilderness of the world? Might this explain your lack of fullness?

Jesus' Essential Message in Seventeen Words

4

MARK 1:14–20 | After John was put in prison, Jesus went into Galilee, proclaiming the good news of God. "The time has come," he said. "The kingdom of God has come near. Repent and believe the good news!"

As Jesus walked beside the Sea of Galilee, he saw Simon and his brother Andrew casting a net into the lake, for they were fishermen. "Come, follow me," Jesus said, "and I will send you out to fish for people." At once they left their nets and followed him.

When he had gone a little farther, he saw James son of Zebedee and his brother John in a boat, preparing their nets. Without delay he called them, and they left their father Zebedee in the boat with the hired men and followed him.

Consider This

Obedience to the Holy Spirit's promptings can land you in jail. In this instance, John made his conviction about marriage known to Herod, who had taken his brother's wife, Herodias; which according to Scripture, constituted adultery. This is the kind of persecution Jesus referenced when he said, "Blessed are those who are persecuted because of righteousness, for theirs is the kingdom of heaven" (Matt. 5:10).

The Holy Spirit keeps the main thing the main thing. Mark clocks in Jesus' first sermon at just under ten seconds. John's core message was every bit of thirty-six words. Jesus cut that in half, coming in at seventeen words. Behold the master-piece: *"The time has come. The kingdom of God has come near. Repent and believe the good news!"*

What is our core essential message? I don't mean you have to be a preacher to have a core message. Your life has one. The question is, What is it? What core essential message is your life—the combination of your words and actions—speaking? Invite the Holy Spirit to clarify this for you. The Holy Spirit will make us an essentialist, to borrow Greg McKeown's term. Life is short. Our message must become clear.

The Holy Spirit prefers lay people. I find it fascinating that Jesus didn't head to the temple to find his followers. Clearly, the most trained and committed religious people in the land were the Scribes and Pharisees. Could it be that sometimes the most educated and trained people have the most unlearning to do when it comes to the life of faith? It is significant that Jesus went to the working world to recruit his disciples. He still does.

The Holy Spirit seems to like preexisting relationships. Our relationships provide the seedbed for the activity of the Holy Spirit. As the person of the Holy Spirit dwells in the unshakable bond between the Father and the Son, so he creates the bonds between the followers of Jesus. The Spirit indwells us individually, but he does so for the sake of our relationships.

Preexisting relationships—two sets of brothers in today's case—offer an out-of-the-box, plug-and-play situation for rapid response. In the best case, there is history, trust, and a framework of tacit understanding between people. In other cases, there's the possibility for healing and reconciliation within broken relationships, which creates an immediate testimony to the work of God.

What if we thought of our present friendships as places where we could invite the Holy Spirit to work for the sake of blessing others? What if we consciously offered our families to God, inviting him to make our relationships therein a place of blessing for others?

The Prayer

Spirit of the living God, fall afresh on me.

The Questions

- Describe the relationships in your life in which the Holy Spirit is working to manifest God's kingdom.
- What relationships have you never considered for this possibility?

5 When I Fight Authority

MARK 1:21–28 ESV | And they went into Capernaum, and immediately on the Sabbath he entered the synagogue and was teaching. And they were astonished at his teaching, for he taught them as one who had authority, and not as the scribes. And immediately there was in their synagogue a man with an unclean spirit. And he cried out, "What have you to do with us, Jesus of Nazareth? Have you come to destroy us? I know who you are—the Holy One of God." But Jesus rebuked him, saying, "Be silent, and come out of him!" And the unclean spirit, convulsing him and crying out with a loud voice, came out of him. And they were all amazed, so that they questioned among themselves, saying, "What is this? A new teaching with authority! He commands even the unclean spirits, and they obey him." And at once his fame spread everywhere throughout all the surrounding region of Galilee.

Consider This

The authority of Jesus is my authority through the gift of the Holy Spirit. Authority is a very interesting concept. First, there are *the* authorities, which typically means the police, as in, "When I fight authority, authority always wins." Then there are people who we refer to as an authority on a particular subject—a respected expert. Then we have leaders who are considered authoritarian, which means they manage to wield a lot of power despite not having any real authority. They tend to be feared more than respected. How about the idea of authorization, which typically refers to a grant or limitation of power, as in, "I'm not authorized to do that." None of this gets at what is meant in today's text where it says, *And they were astonished at his teaching, for he taught them as one who had authority, and not as the scribes.*

The teachers of the law were recognized authorities who operated within a certain bandwidth of religious authorization. They could be considered an authority on all matters pertaining to Scripture and its application to life. They more or less earned their authority by their legal righteousness. Jesus saw right through them. He referred to them as hypocrites— they maintained the appearance of righteousness but inside they were corrupt.

This cuts to the heart of the nature of Jesus' authority. It was unlike theirs in that his authority proceeded from the endless depths of his authenticity. True authority is the fruit of real authenticity. This is why true authority can always be trusted. The hallmark of true authority is humility. This is what it means to be a real Christian.

Let me cut to the bottom line. Authority cannot be earned. The more a person tries to earn authority the more they prove they do not possess it. In fact, authority is not something you possess. Authority is who you become, and the only way there is the path of authenticity. Here's where I will get controversial. The only way to true authenticity is through the only truly authentic One—Jesus of Nazareth, the Messiah. He is the image of the invisible God, the one in whose image we were created and through whom we are becoming new creations.

Jesus doesn't have authority, nor is he "an" authority, nor is he "the" authority. He *is* Authority Incarnate—Word made Flesh—very God of very God. And he gives authority to those who will give themselves to him.

> "All authority in heaven and on earth has been given to me. Therefore go and make disciples of all nations, baptizing them in the name of the Father and of the Son and of the Holy Spirit, and teaching them to obey everything I have commanded you. And surely I am with you always, to the very end of the age." (Matt. 28:18–20)

The authority of Jesus becomes the authority of his followers through the authenticity of their fellowship in the Holy Spirit. The Holy Spirit authenticates the sons and daughters of God by making them truly human; which is to say, the humble image-bearers of the Son of God.

Will you dare to make this claim? "The authority of Jesus is my authority through the gift of the Holy Spirit." Now claim it aloud. "The authority of Jesus is my authority through the gift of the Holy Spirit." One more time: "The authority of Jesus is my authority through the gift of the Holy Spirit."

It's a humbling reality, isn't it?

The Prayer

Spirit of the living God, fall afresh on me.

The Questions

- Think of and describe a person in your past or present who carries the humble authority of Jesus. What is it about them?

Bringing the Holy Spirit Home

6

MARK 1:29–34 NRSV | As soon as they left the synagogue, they entered the house of Simon and Andrew, with James and John. Now Simon's mother-in-law was in bed with a fever, and they told him about her at once. He came and took her by the hand and lifted her up. Then the fever left her, and she began to serve them.

That evening, at sunset, they brought to him all who were sick or possessed with demons. And the whole city was gathered around the door. And he cured many who were sick with various diseases, and cast out many demons; and he would not permit the demons to speak, because they knew him.

Consider This

I believe Jesus intends his church to look a lot more like the scene at Simon's home than the synagogue. The whole town didn't gather at the synagogue. The whole town gathered at the door of Simon's home. I don't want to diminish the importance of church buildings where people gather, yet I do want to emphasize the importance of understanding our homes as places of church and to acknowledge our neighborhoods are filled with people who are sick, lonely, demon possessed and oppressed, depressed, and anxious. These people are far more likely to encounter Jesus in our homes than in our church buildings. It has been said you may be the only Bible some people ever read. It is also true that your home may be the only church some people will ever enter. What would it mean for our homes to have the magnetic appeal of the presence of the Holy Spirit?

Wherever the Holy Spirit is actively working, there you have the church. But it does not follow that just because we call what we are doing "church" that the Holy Spirit is actively working there. I have a close friend who is a leader of a seminary in Russia. On one occasion he told me that if the Holy Spirit was not active in a local church community in Russia there was no way to get people to come. He said you could give away food and clothes and even money and still people wouldn't come. However, he said, if the Holy Spirit was actively working in a local church community you couldn't keep people away. He said they would fight their way in if necessary. That's how I imagine the scene that evening at Simon's home.

The same is true today. You don't have to invite people to places where the Holy Spirit is actively at work. In fact, you can't keep them away.

We are way too in the box when it comes to the Holy Spirit and the active work of Jesus Christ in the world. We tend to think it only really happens in church services. All the emphasis goes on getting the music right, cultivating the mood and feel of the room, and preaching a message designed to evoke a response. What if the bigger possibilities lived around the places we spent our six days instead of so much focus on what happens during one hour a week? What if our homes became the primary locus of church? I don't know about you, but I'm not actively praying for my neighbors and plotting ways I can do good for them. It just hasn't occurred to me. It's time to kindle the fire of the Holy Spirit in our homes.

What if our homes held the spiritual significance of the burning bush—on fire but not consumed; holy ground with a welcome mat?

The Prayer
Spirit of the living God, fall afresh on me.

The Questions
- When and where is the last time you witnessed or experienced church beyond the building you call the church? What happened?

The Most Important Word in the New Testament

7

MARK 1:35–42 | Very early in the morning, while it was still dark, Jesus got up, left the house and went off to a solitary place, where he prayed. Simon and his companions went to look for him, and when they found him, they exclaimed: "Everyone is looking for you!"

Jesus replied, "Let us go somewhere else—to the nearby villages—so I can preach there also. That is why I have come." So he traveled throughout Galilee, preaching in their synagogues and driving out demons.

A man with leprosy came to him and begged him on his knees, "If you are willing, you can make me clean."

Jesus was indignant. He reached out his hand and touched the man. "I am willing," he said. "Be clean!" Immediately the leprosy left him and he was cleansed.

Consider This

As it was with Jesus, so it is ever becoming with his followers. How can I say this? I want us to remember an earth-shattering statement Jesus made to his disciples about the Holy Spirit in John's gospel, "Very truly I tell you, whoever believes in me will do the works I have been doing, and they will do even greater things than these, because I am going to the Father" (John 14:12).

There are many places on planet Earth today where this word from Jesus is being fulfilled. Unfortunately, there are many more places where it is not being fulfilled. I suspect if you are reading the Daily Text, you find yourself in one of those places where this is not happening so much.

"Because I am going to the Father" is a direct reference to the Holy Spirit, who was sent by the Father and the Son ten days after Jesus' ascent into heaven (see Acts 1–2).

The first question we must ask ourselves is: Do I want to be in one of those places on planet Earth where John 14:12 is being fulfilled? If the answer is no, pray in earnest one of our favorite Daily Text prayers: "Lord Jesus Christ, have mercy on me, a sinner."

If the answer is yes, we have two basic choices. Choice #1: We can relocate ourselves to one of those places in the world where John 14:12 is happening. Choice #2: We can make some game-changing, life-altering adjustments that hold the potential for the fulfillment of John 14:12 right where we live.

I'm proceeding under the assumption that you, like me, have probably chosen Choice #2. If so, we need to deal with one of the major pitfalls of this choice.

We must move from a faith built on functionalism to a faith founded in fellowship. In John 14:12, the Greek word for "believe" is πιστεύω (transliterated as *pisteuó* and phonetically pronounced as "pist-yoo-o"). It is arguably one of the most significant words in the New Testament, and one of the most misunderstood.

There are two primary ways we misunderstand this concept. First, we tend to think the word "believe" means an intellectual assent to the truth of something. For instance, many people claim to believe what the Bible says, yet they have no idea what it says. They assent to its truth. This is not what the New Testament means when it speaks of believing in something. To believe is not the same thing as having beliefs.

Second, we think of belief as a kind of lever that we pull in order to make something else happen. Faith is treated as a functional reality. If I do this, then God will do that. For instance, people often treat prayer this way—it's a means to an end. If we pray, then God will act. This is the essence of the prosperity gospel, which is just another form of idolatry. If we can get enough faith or enough people praying or giving or whatever else we get cajoled to do in the name of Jesus, then God will do what God does. It's the essence of deal-making. There is a lot of Scripture that gets deployed to prove this approach, but it's a fundamental misunderstanding of the way God works.

Today's text shows us a picture of *pisteuó* (belief or faith) in action. Jesus' practice of waking early and going to a solitary place to pray shows us faith founded in fellowship. This is not his secret to getting things done later in the day. This is his life. Jesus is meeting with his Father in the fellowship of the Holy Spirit, and though it changes format depending on the situation at hand, he does it all day long. Jesus gives us a lesson on this in John 15. The word "abide" is shorthand for "fellowship with the Holy Spirit."

Fellowship with the Holy Spirit is what gets Jesus up in the morning. It's what moves him through his days. It is from this fellowship that lepers are cleansed. It's what gives him sleep at night. It is into this fellowship that he invites us to join. And, remember, as it was with Jesus, so it is becoming with us. Right?

I'll give Paul the last word today with this blessing, "May the grace of the Lord Jesus Christ, and the love of God, and the fellowship of the Holy Spirit be with you all" (2 Cor. 13:14).

The Prayer

Spirit of the living God, fall afresh on me.

The Questions

- What is your experience of the fellowship of the Holy Spirit?
- Do you struggle with flatness of faith?

8 The Difference between Witnessing and Being a Witness

MARK 1:43–45 ESV | And Jesus sternly charged him and sent him away at once, and said to him, "See that you say nothing to anyone, but go, show yourself to the priest and offer for your cleansing what Moses commanded, for a proof to them." But he went out and began to talk freely about it, and to spread the news, so that Jesus could no longer openly enter a town, but was out in desolate places, and people were coming to him from every quarter.

Consider This

When a person experiences the work of the Holy Spirit, as this leper did, they will tell others about it. It's that simple. No one has to tell them to spread the news. I am convinced human beings were created to spread good news.

It's interesting how hard churches work to motivate people to witness to other people about their faith. They want us to tell others about Jesus, to lead others to Christ, and so on. Don't get me wrong. Those are great things, but we go about it in the wrong way. At the end of the day, all this activity adds up to is marketing.

You can't talk people into being a witness. Really you can't even teach or train them to be a witness. A witness actually has to witness something happening in order to be a witness. A witness is a witness by virtue of something they have experienced. Sure, we can get people to do marketing for Jesus, but that's a far cry from actually being a witness to his work through the person and power of the Holy Spirit.

Not even Jesus could stop this leper from spreading the news about what happened. Our best marketing efforts can fill the seats of our sanctuaries, but getting people to talk freely and spread the news about Jesus—that only happens when the Holy Spirit does the work of Jesus within them.

Jesus said, "But you will receive power when the Holy Spirit has come upon you and you will be my witnesses . . ." (Acts 1:8). I think he had in mind something of the scene in today's text—the unstoppable sharing of the good news of the God who turns everything around. We live in a day when the gospel has been reduced to information about God that we should feel compelled to share with other people, and we call that evangelism. Real evangelism looks like witnesses telling stories in such a way that the people who hear them flock to the countryside in search of Jesus. Jesus can't even get past crowd control to get into the building. Because of the witness to the Holy Spirit's work in and through him, he can't even get into the towns. People hate marketing for Jesus. They hunger for witnesses who will tell stories of what the Holy Spirit is doing through the people of God in the name of Jesus.

What if this actually happens better and more often on the outskirts of town, in the lonely places, than in our Sunday morning worship services?

The Prayer

Spirit of the living God, fall afresh on me.

The Questions

- Can you draw a distinction between marketing and being a witness in your own life? In your walk with God?
- What have you witnessed of the Spirit's working?

9 When the Holy Spirit Makes a Hot Mess

MARK 2:1–12 NRSV | When he returned to Capernaum after some days, it was reported that he was at home. So many gathered around that there was no longer room for them, not even in front of the door; and he was speaking the word to them. Then some people came, bringing to him a paralyzed man, carried by four of them. And when they could not bring him to Jesus because of the crowd, they removed the roof above him; and after having dug through it, they let down the mat on which the paralytic lay. When Jesus saw their faith, he said to the paralytic, "Son, your sins are forgiven." Now some of the scribes were sitting there, questioning in their hearts, "Why does this fellow speak in this way? It is blasphemy! Who can forgive sins but God alone?" At once Jesus perceived in his spirit that they were discussing these questions among themselves; and he said to them, "Why do you raise such questions in your hearts? Which is easier, to say to the paralytic, 'Your sins are forgiven,' or to say, 'Stand up and take your mat and walk'? But so that you may know that the Son of Man has authority on earth to forgive sins"—he said to the paralytic—"I say to you, stand up, take your mat and go to your home." And he stood up, and immediately took the mat and went out before all of them; so that they were all amazed and glorified God, saying, "We have never seen anything like this!"

Consider This

When the Holy Spirit is at work, things will get messy. It's so easy to look back on this story and see those four guys who brought their friend to Jesus as heroes. Try to put yourself in that room. Jesus was "speaking the word to them," so the text says. All of a sudden, the roof starts caving in.

They made an opening in the roof above Jesus by digging through it. This was a show stopper; a major disturbance. Imagine you are at your local church and Billy Graham is the guest preacher. He's right in the middle of his mesmerizing message when four people burst through the doors carrying a handicapped derelict beggar, putting him down right in front of the pulpit where Dr. Graham is preaching. He can do nothing but stop his message and deal with the situation at hand. This would be maddening to everyone gathered. It would be an embarrassment to them.

What happened that day in Capernaum was a major disturbance of the gathering. Take it a step further and put yourself in the position of the guy who owned the house.

He now needed a major roof repair. Think about the crowd gathered four people deep outside of the house, pressing to get in, tiptoeing to see the Son of God and craning their necks to hear what he was saying. These guys carrying the paralytic not only stopped the show inside the house, they cut in line—big time. They didn't have a ticket or take a number. They skipped. That's a foul. Did they not realize that other people could have brought their sick friends, too, had they known this was that kind of event?

This was not a warm, fuzzy devotional moment. Sure, everybody was amazed in the end—but at the time it had to be an unwelcome, big, fat, hot mess. When the Holy Spirit is at work, things can get pretty messy, even out of hand. Unplanned and unpredictable stuff happens. We have to learn to see through all that to the greater thing God may be doing.

Jesus saw straight through the fracas and spots the faith. He saw their faith. My hunch? There was only one person present that day who was glad for the mess being made by these four interlopers and their paralyzed friend—Jesus.

When Jesus saw their faith, he said to the paralytic, "Son, your sins are forgiven."

Sometimes our friends must have faith for us and sometimes that's enough. Jesus didn't see the faith of the paralyzed man. He saw the faith of his friends. There's that word again for faith: πίστις "pistis." Faith is not about our beliefs. It's about our believing. Those friends were believing in Jesus on behalf of their friend in need. Can we have faith for someone

This is why we pray for each other.

28

else? Absolutely. Jesus loves it when that happens. That's what love looks like.

The Prayer

Spirit of the living God, fall afresh on me.

The Questions

- Think back through your past. Can you remember anyone who had faith for you?
- Who in your life right now are you having faith for? Are there friends you are conspiring with to get someone else to Jesus?

Why There Is No Such Thing as Secular

10

MARK 2:13–17 | Once again Jesus went out beside the lake. A large crowd came to him, and he began to teach them. As he walked along, he saw Levi son of Alphaeus sitting at the tax collector's booth. "Follow me," Jesus told him, and Levi got up and followed him.

While Jesus was having dinner at Levi's house, many tax collectors and sinners were eating with him and his disciples, for there were many who followed him. When the teachers of the law who were Pharisees saw him eating with the sinners and tax collectors, they asked his disciples: "Why does he eat with tax collectors and sinners?"

On hearing this, Jesus said to them, "It is not the healthy who need a doctor, but the sick. I have not come to call the righteous, but sinners."

Consider This

The ministry of the Holy Spirit collapses the compartmentalized categories of sacred and secular, church and world, sanctuary and streets. Jesus does the overwhelming majority of his work right in the middle of the everyday world—where everybody else is doing their everyday work. The Holy Spirit doesn't seem to be in search of religious facilities. Jesus spends his days next to the Sea of Galilee, in the host of towns and villages around the sea, in the homes of tax collectors, sinners, and friends. By comparison he goes to the synagogue once a week and hardly ever visits the Big House (a.k.a. the temple).

We tend to think the Holy Spirit mostly works when people gather in the church building. We observe the opposite in the ministry of Jesus—the Holy Spirit mostly works where people live out their lives in the work-a-day world. Jesus is not creating environments for seekers. He is going out and seeking them where they live and work. The Holy Spirit breaks the "you come to us" approach, putting in its place the "we go to you" method.

Jesus constantly shows us what it looks like when the Holy Spirit works through a person to enter desecrated places and

Jesus & the Holy Spirit is an everyday Thing.

restore their sacred character. It reminds me of a line in one of my favorite Wendell Berry poems, "How to Be a Poet": "There are no unsacred places; there are only sacred places and desecrated places."

Jesus is drawn to desecrated people and places with magnetic force. He touches a desecrated leper and restores his sacredness. He approaches a despised tax collector and restores his sacredness as a called one of God.

When sin touches the sacred, it becomes desecrated. When the Sacred One touches the desecrated ones, the desecrated ones become sacred again. This is what got him in so much trouble with the religious authorities, whose work was to maintain the boundaries between the clean and unclean, the sinners and the righteous and to enforce the boundaries between the sacred and secular.

In today's text we see Jesus in the home of a tax collector seated around the table with a crowd of notorious sinners. It looks to the religious authorities that he is affirming sin. It makes no sense to them.

When the teachers of the law who were Pharisees saw him eating with the sinners and tax collectors, they asked his disciples: "Why does he eat with tax collectors and sinners?"

The truth? Jesus hates sin because sin desecrates all he has created. He loves sinners and he is willing to walk right into the heart of sin, even if it looks bad; even if he gets accused of going soft on crime, because he loves sinners that much. He doesn't care what it looks like. In fact, he is willing to risk being misunderstood as affirming sin in order to carry out his mission of restoring desecrated sinners into the sacred sons and daughters of God.

I think this is the kind of risk-taking he's looking for from his followers. The Holy Spirit is always ready to empower those risk-takers. Yes, they will often pay a price, but those are the ones Jesus will be high-fiving in the end.

Am I so comfortable & only see the good ones

The Prayer

Spirit of the living God, fall afresh on me.

The Questions

- How much have you permitted the world around you to draw lines separating the secular and the sacred in your way of seeing people and things? How might you redraw those lines?

11 What Makes Fasting Christian?

MARK 2:18–22 ESV | Now John's disciples and the Pharisees were fasting. And people came and said to him, "Why do John's disciples and the disciples of the Pharisees fast, but your disciples do not fast?" And Jesus said to them, "Can the wedding guests fast while the bridegroom is with them? As long as they have the bridegroom with them, they cannot fast. The days will come when the bridegroom is taken away from them, and then they will fast in that day. No one sews a piece of unshrunk cloth on an old garment. If he does, the patch tears away from it, the new from the old, and a worse tear is made. And no one puts new wine into old wineskins. If he does, the wine will burst the skins—and the wine is destroyed, and so are the skins. But new wine is for fresh wineskins."

Consider This

Fasting is not unique to Christianity, but Christian fasting is unique. In today's text, John's disciples are fasting and the Pharisees are fasting. Everybody seems to be fasting, except Jesus and his disciples. So what's the difference? Why weren't Jesus' disciples fasting? I think the difference has to do with the Holy Spirit.

Jesus indicated fasting would not be appropriate for his disciples as long as he was with them. Fasting would begin when Jesus ascended into heaven. My theory? For Jesus, fasting was about cultivating fellowship. As long as he had this face-to-face fellowship with his followers there would be no need to fast. Fasting would be necessary later to cultivate fellowship with Jesus (despite his physical absence) through the presence of the Holy Spirit.

For other religions, fasting seems more to be about faithfulness than fellowship. Why do Muslims fast? Fasting is one of the five pillars of Islam. They do it to be faithful to the requirements of their faith. Ramadan, the annual Muslim period of fasting, begins June 17 and runs through July 17. They will forego eating all day long and feast every night. Fasting for John's disciples and fasting for the Pharisees seems also to be about faithfulness to religious duty. It's a way to signal you are taking your religion seriously. It seems they surmised Jesus' disciples were being less than faithful because they weren't fasting. For Jesus, fasting was not about faithfulness. Fasting was a means to intimate fellowship.

Now to this business of wine and wineskins. I have never understood the meaning of these sayings concerning new wine and old wineskins. Only now am I even coming close to possibly approaching an insight. What if fasting for the sake of religious duty and faithfulness is the old wineskin? And what if the new wine is the Holy Spirit? Wouldn't it make sense that the old wineskins of duty-bound religious fasting could not contain the new wine of the fellowship of the Holy Spirit? Wouldn't this call for a new kind of fasting; fasting not for the duty of faithfulness to God but for the purpose of fellowship with God? What if fasting is about focusing our attune-ment on the Holy Spirit for the sake of abiding in Jesus?

This notion of fellowship beyond faithfulness also resonates with Jesus' words to his disciples in the Sermon on the Mount: "But when you fast, anoint your head and wash your face, that your fasting may not be seen by others but by your Father who is in secret. And your Father who sees in secret will reward you" (Matt. 6:17–18 ESV).

Fasting is about the hidden delights of fellowship over public demonstrations of faithfulness.

Fasting give time for prayer
Teaches Self-discipline
Reminds us we can do with a lot less
Appreciates God's gift

34

THE GOSPEL OF THE HOLY SPIRIT

The Prayer

Spirit of the living God, fall afresh on me.

The Questions

- Are you fasting with any regularity?
- If so, how might this insight about fellowship with the Holy Spirit encourage you? If not, would you like to grow in your fellowship with Jesus in the Holy Spirit?

Ready for the New Wine? Get Rid of the Old Wineskin

12

MARK 2:23–28 NRSV | One sabbath he was going through the grainfields; and as they made their way his disciples began to pluck heads of grain. The Pharisees said to him, "Look, why are they doing what is not lawful on the sabbath?" And he said to them, "Have you never read what David did when he and his companions were hungry and in need of food? He entered the house of God, when Abiathar was high priest, and ate the bread of the Presence, which it is not lawful for any but the priests to eat, and he gave some to his companions." Then he said to them, "The sabbath was made for humankind, and not humankind for the sabbath; so the Son of Man is lord even of the sabbath."

Consider This

Could Sabbath be another wineskin issue? Yesterday it was about fasting. Today it's about food. Once again, the so-called faithful are concerned about enforcing faithfulness to the law as it relates to Sabbath-keeping. Jesus' disciples were hungry and they plucked a few heads of grain to cut their appetite. The Pharisees appeal to the rules. Jesus appealed to the purpose of the rules—real people (i.e., David).

Old wineskins: man was made for the Sabbath.

New wineskins: the Sabbath was made for man.

Old wineskins were about getting it right.

New wineskins are about keeping it real.

Old wineskins were about external appearance.

New wineskins are about internal identity.

Old wineskins were about fulfilling duty.

New wineskins are about training desire.

Old wineskins: fasting is all about faithfulness.

New wineskins: fasting is all about fellowship.

Old wineskins: Sabbath is all about prohibitions.

New wineskins: Sabbath is all about provision.

The issue is not about the practice, but the purpose. The old way: perfecting performance through religious practice. The new way: perfecting purpose through practicing love. The Holy Spirit is not in search of perfect people. The Holy Spirit searches for people whom he can perfect in love.

Old wineskins: keeping it religious.

New wineskins: keeping it authentic.

So what about the new wine? That's the Holy Spirit. Remember the day of Pentecost, when the Holy Spirit first descended on the apostles? Remember what the people said? "And all were amazed and perplexed, saying to one another, 'What does this mean?' But others sneered and said, 'They are filled with new wine'" (Acts 2:12–13 NRSV). *The Holy Spirit*

Jesus' agenda for his disciples: stripping away the old wineskins of a religious kind of holy to make way for the new wineskins of a human kind of holy. It's not an easy transition. The pathway must go through the cross.

Ready for the new wine of the Holy Spirit? Keep it real.

The Prayer
Spirit of the living God, fall afresh on me.

The Questions
- Do you tend to be more stuck in the old wineskin mentality or are you guilty of throwing out the baby with the bathwater on things like fasting and Sabbath-keeping?
- What might a new wineskin approach look like for you?

The old was obeying the laws. The New is getting to know Jesus And His Love through the Holy Spirit — Loving your Neighbor as Jesus loves you. Jesus teaching were for a New world learning what he did - putting it into action.

37

13

The Critical Difference between Being Responsible *for* Others and Responsive *to* Them

MARK 3:1–6 | Another time Jesus went into the synagogue, and a man with a shriveled hand was there. Some of them were looking for a reason to accuse Jesus, so they watched him closely to see if he would heal him on the Sabbath. Jesus said to the man with the shriveled hand, "Stand up in front of everyone."

Then Jesus asked them, "Which is lawful on the Sabbath: to do good or to do evil, to save life or to kill?" But they remained silent.

He looked around at them in anger and, deeply distressed at their stubborn hearts, said to the man, "Stretch out your hand." He stretched it out, and his hand was completely restored. Then the Pharisees went out and began to plot with the Herodians how they might kill Jesus.

Consider This

The Holy Spirit always brings life. Always. When the Holy Spirit inhabits a person, the person becomes a force for goodness and life. We see this in perfection through the life of Jesus.

What does it look like when the Holy Spirit fills our spirit? Jesus reveals this to us in complete perfection. No matter where Jesus goes, the Holy Spirit constantly alerts him to human need. In today's text, Jesus enters the synagogue and immediately notices the man with the withered hand. In fact, everywhere he goes he notices people in need.

Children have a hard time looking away from people in need. The older we get, though, the easier it is to block them out. Why? Because we feel burdened by the needs of others. And herein lies the problem. We make the mistake of thinking we are responsible for other people, and because we can't carry that burden, we protect ourselves from them. The easiest way to do this is to simply stop noticing them.

What if we stopped feeling responsible *for* other people in need and began to approach them with the simple question of how the Holy Spirit might want to be responsive *to* their need through us? Sometimes, it's as simple as seeing them as a fellow broken human being and not just a human need.

I don't know about you, but when it comes to helping other people, I feel extremely limited in my capacity. In becoming a human being, God, who has no limitations, severely limited himself. Jesus was fully God and yet he was a single person and thereby accordingly limited. He could only be in one place in one time and he could only engage with a limited number of people each day. As a single human being he could not be present to the entire human race, but he could be profoundly responsive to the people he was with—and he was.

How can I be more Responsive?
Do I Not listen to the Holy Spirit.

39

It gets better. A single person on an ordinary Friday is lifted up on a single cross and buried in a single tomb and is raised from the dead and ascends into heaven. He sent the Holy Spirit and as a result of this singular event, an unlimited number of people can receive the gift of salvation and eternal life.

Something happens when we become profoundly present to another person in the fellowship of the Holy Spirit. Human limitations become transcended by divine Presence. The power of this not only blesses the recipient but also the giver, and beyond that, the blessing extends to everyone who ever hears about it. Think about the impact these stories about Jesus are having on us two thousand years later.

People regularly write me and tell me stories along these lines about a person from their present or who has long since passed who was responsive to them in a very human way that had a divine impact. Every time these stories are told, it's like the miracle happens all over again.

The guy with the withered hand? He had no idea what would come of that day.

The Prayer

Spirit of the living God, fall afresh on me.

The Questions

- What would it mean for you to be less responsible for other people and more responsive to them?

The World —

If You Had a Holy Spirit Gauge, What Would It Read?

14

MARK 3:7–12 ESV | Jesus withdrew with his disciples to the sea, and a great crowd followed, from Galilee and Judea and Jerusalem and Idumea and from beyond the Jordan and from around Tyre and Sidon. When the great crowd heard all that he was doing, they came to him. And he told his disciples to have a boat ready for him because of the crowd, lest they crush him, for he had healed many, so that all who had diseases pressed around him to touch him. And whenever the unclean spirits saw him, they fell down before him and cried out, "You are the Son of God." And he strictly ordered them not to make him known.

Consider This

We supposedly only use about 10 percent of the capacity of our brain. On a similar note, what if we could flip a switch that told us the percentage to which the Holy Spirit was filling us at any given moment. What would your gauge read?

Doesn't it make sense? If a person can be filled with the Holy Spirit, they can also be half full or even running on empty.

We know Jesus' gauge read 100 percent all the time. Scripture says the Spirit dwelled in him even beyond measure. That is why the crowds of people were irresistibly drawn to him as we see in today's text. It's also why, as the text reveals, the demonic spirits *"fell down before him and cried out, 'You are the Son of God.'"*

I think this is the essence of what becoming a disciple of Jesus is all about. It's learning from him what it means and what it takes to move the needle on our Holy Spirit gauge. Learning to walk in the humble way of the cross means learning to live in the powerful way of the Holy Spirit. This is not about a formula, but a fellowship. It's not the love of power, but the power of love. It takes an ever-deepening maturity characterized by an ever-present humility to grasp this.

There is always more of the Holy Spirit. The issue is the level of our availability—that's the percentage to which we will be filled with the Holy Spirit. This is what the means of grace are all about—deepening our fellowship with Jesus through the personal presence of the Holy Spirit. What if we aren't witnessing New Testament realities because we have anemic levels of the fullness of the Holy Spirit?

Even more interesting is the way Jesus gave the demons strict orders not to tell anyone about him. Jesus exercised authority over the principalities and powers of darkness.

What if one's level of kingdom authority cannot exceed their level of Holy Spirit fullness? It would make sense of the seeming sway of the powers of darkness in our time. I don't want to be over simplistic with these lines of thinking, yet I do want to explore the hypothesis.

The Prayer

Spirit of the living God, fall afresh on me.

The Questions

- On a scale of 1–10, with 10 being full, where do you sense your own level of fullness of the Holy Spirit?
- What might be a way to move that level upward?

The Missing Link in Our Disciple-Making

15

MARK 3:13–19 NRSV | He went up the mountain and called to him those whom he wanted, and they came to him. And he appointed twelve, whom he also named apostles, to be with him, and to be sent out to proclaim the message, and to have authority to cast out demons. So he appointed the twelve: Simon (to whom he gave the name Peter); James son of Zebedee and John the brother of James (to whom he gave the name Boanerges, that is, Sons of Thunder); and Andrew, and Philip, and Bartholomew, and Matthew, and Thomas, and James son of Alphaeus, and Thaddaeus, and Simon the Cananaean, and Judas Iscariot, who betrayed him.

Consider This

And he appointed twelve . . . to be with him. I think this is where we miss it in today's typical church discipleship ministries. We are good with appointing people to get involved in the work of the church. We excel at getting people on committees and boards and even ministry teams. We send them out to teach and preach; not so much when it comes to driving out demons. Come to think of it, we can be pretty clear about the necessity of "be[ing] with him," Jesus, in a personal relationship.

The thing we have lost is this practice of appointing people that they might "be with [us]." If we are following the Holy Spirit's pattern with respect to making disciples, we will follow Jesus' example and appoint others to be with us. It sounds audacious and perhaps even prideful. After all, who am I to appoint others to be with me? The big point, however, is in being with me (or you), they are actually with Jesus in me (or you).

This is the purpose of his calling the Twelve to be with him, so they could in turn appoint others to be with them in the same fashion. In fact we wouldn't be here were it not for this apostolic appointment process proceeding from then until this very day.

Making disciples happens in fellowship. It requires being together over the course of time. Discipleship can't be reduced to the transfer of information; nor can it be simply going through the right training regime or getting the right education. Making disciples begins with the appointment to be with another person and to enjoy the fellowship of the Holy Spirit with other people over a period of time.

Jesus is not calling me to appoint people to be with him. What if he's actually appointing others to be with himself through me? Through you? It would behoove us to discern who those people may be and invite them to share in the fellowship of the Holy Spirit with us.

Discipleship isn't this program or that small group. It's a life rich in the Word of God and the Holy Spirit shared in a day-in and day-out ordinary life context with other people.

Being together with him is not a means to another end either. It is *the* means and *the* end. Discipleship cultivates a context of holy friendship wherein the authority of Jesus is shared among us for the benefit and blessing of others. Authority is not a transactional reality. It is a community dynamic. Soon Jesus will be sending out these disciples two by two. It's our discipled relationships lived out in the fellowship of the Holy Spirit that create the context for the exercise of kingdom-of-God authority for the love of the world.

So often authority gets couched in terms of enforcement of the law. Jesus turned that on its ear. For Jesus and his followers, authority became the license and empowerment to help people.

While driving through a fairly rough and run-down part of Shreveport, Louisiana, I came across what looked like an oasis. It was some kind of church. The sign said, "The 'From Bondage to Freedom' Victory Center."

Wow! I thought to myself. *What would it be like to work there?* I could imagine a pastor colleague asking me, "So, where do you serve?" I would reply, "I work down at "The 'From Bondage to Freedom' Victory Center," and you?" He or she might look down at their feet and say, "Uhhh, I work down at First Methodist."

Friends—we serve at "The 'From Bondage to Freedom' Victory Center"! That's the kind of authority we share in.

Ready to go to work? *Bondage of the world,*

The Prayer

Spirit of the living God, fall afresh on me.

The Questions

- Can you remember a time or season in your life when you found yourself in real fellowship of discipleship? What was that like?

16 | Three Reasons You Have Probably Not Blasphemed the Holy Spirit

MARK 3:20–30 | Then Jesus entered a house, and again a crowd gathered, so that he and his disciples were not even able to eat. When his family heard about this, they went to take charge of him, for they said, "He is out of his mind."

And the teachers of the law who came down from Jerusalem said, "He is possessed by Beelzebul! By the prince of demons he is driving out demons."

So Jesus called them over to him and began to speak to them in parables: "How can Satan drive out Satan? If a kingdom is divided against itself, that kingdom cannot stand. If a house is divided against itself, that house cannot stand. And if Satan opposes himself and is divided, he cannot stand; his end has come. In fact, no one can enter a strong man's house without first tying him up. Then he can plunder the strong man's house. Truly I tell you, people can be forgiven all their sins and every slander they utter, but whoever blasphemes against the Holy Spirit will never be forgiven; they are guilty of an eternal sin."

He said this because they were saying, "He has an impure spirit."

Consider This

What on earth does it mean to blaspheme the Holy Spirit? It's been something of the sixty-four-thousand-dollar question across the centuries. It makes sense. Who wouldn't want to know the one sin Jesus says is unpardonable? That's one we would want to steer very clear of.

So what does it mean to blaspheme the Holy Spirit? Some think it means to renounce God or to curse God. I don't think so. Jesus' words as recorded in Matthew's gospel put it this way, "Anyone who speaks a word against the Son of Man will be forgiven, but anyone who speaks against the Holy Spirit

Conscious and hardened opposition to the truth. Because the Spirit is truth. Leads man away from humility & Repentance. Without Repentance.

will not be forgiven, either in this age or in the age to come"
(Matt. 12:32). *There can be No forgiveNess*

Based on today's text and the one just cited, my holding is that blaspheming against the Holy Spirit means attributing the work of the Holy Spirit to Satan. Jesus seems to be issuing a stern warning to the people who just attributed the Spirit's work through him to Beelzebul, a.k.a. Satan.

Scripture speaks of quenching the Holy Spirit, grieving the Holy Spirit, resisting the Holy Spirit, all of which are pardonable. Blaspheming the Holy Spirit, on the other hand, cannot be forgiven.

I will always remember a particular kid in my youth group who was utterly convinced he had committed the unpardonable sin. Interestingly enough, for my money, this kid loved God more than all the rest of the other kids put together. In retrospect, the big problem was he had no concept of what blaspheming the Holy Spirit meant.

Most of you reading may find this one of the less engaging Daily Text entries. However, there are likely two or three readers who are gravely concerned that they may have blasphemed the Holy Spirit somewhere along the way. I would like to put your mind at ease. (1) The fact you are concerned you have committed the unpardonable sin is probably the best sign that you have not done so. (2) Blaspheming the Holy Spirit requires a level of intent and willfulness such that you would have no doubt you had done it. In other words, it's not the kind of thing a person wonders if they have done or not. (3) Finally, the kind of person who blasphemes the Holy Spirit is not the kind of person who is worried about it.

The Prayer

Spirit of the living God, fall afresh on me.

The Questions

- Have you ever wondered about the unpardonable sin and whether you have committed it?
- Have you ever known others who have struggled with this?

Why Jesus Is the New (Old) Normal

17

MARK 3:31–35 ESV | And his mother and his brothers came, and standing outside they sent to him and called him. And a crowd was sitting around him, and they said to him, "Your mother and your brothers are outside, seeking you." And he answered them, "Who are my mother and my brothers?" And looking about at those who sat around him, he said, "Here are my mother and my brothers! For whoever does the will of God, he is my brother and sister and mother." *Jesus was baptised by John God called out you are my*

Consider This *son whom I am please*

Jesus is the new normal. So where does the idea of normal come from? Let's take this back to the garden. God's original image-bearers, the paradigmatic human beings, made in his image, represent the norm for the human race. The big problem for the human race from the first people to

49

you and me is we have forsaken normal and exchanged it for abnormal instead. Sin, death, and all the brokenness in between are not normal. Over the course of millennia now, sin has become normalized. Why else would we so readily accept it as the inevitable consequence of being human. And the truth—because of the choice of our forbearers, sin and death became the default condition of the human race. Sin is our fallen condition, but it is not normal.

After this line of argument, it strikes me now to suggest Jesus is not the new normal. Jesus is the old normal. How about we just say Jesus is the norm. And this is the big issue. We don't consider Jesus the norm. We typically think of him as an impossible standard bearer. We consider sin, brokenness, and death as the norm. And the big problem with norms is they rarely get challenged. In fact, anytime the norms are challenged, the challenger meets extraordinary resistance. Just ask Jesus.

The religious elite thought he was abnormal; going so far as to say he was of Satan. Even his family thought he was abnormal. Family systems and religious structures are some of the most powerful norm-enforcing entities on the planet. Jesus departed from the religious script. He departed from the family script. And anyone who has ever done either of those things knows what happens. They will do whatever lies within their power to bring you back in line. Interestingly enough, it often looks like some form of tantrum.

Jesus reforms religious structures and reframes family systems. On the former, look what he has said so far about fasting and Sabbath and the kingdom of God, and the list will grow as we proceed through the story. On families, he put it pretty plainly when he said, *"For whoever does the will of God, he is my brother and sister and mother."*

If there's one thing we can be sure of, it's that the world's vision of normal is a moving target. It's constantly changing. There's always a so-called new normal. With Jesus, normal is as fixed as the sun. He is our norm. Because of the Holy Spirit, his life is our possibility and it's the most normal thing in all creation.

The Prayer

Spirit of the living God, fall afresh on me.

The Questions

- How deeply have you normalized the abnormal realities of sin and death in your life?
- What might adopting the new normal of Jesus and the Spirit-filled life look like?

How to Have a High Failure Rate without Failing

18

MARK 4:1–9 NRSV | Again he began to teach beside the sea. Such a very large crowd gathered around him that he got into a boat on the sea and sat there, while the whole crowd was beside the sea on the land. He began to teach them many things in parables, and in his teaching he said to them: "Listen! A sower went out to sow. And as he sowed, some seed fell on the path, and the birds came and ate it up. Other seed fell on rocky ground, where it did not have much soil, and it sprang up quickly, since it had no depth of soil. And when the sun rose, it was scorched; and since it had no root, it withered away. Other seed fell among thorns, and the thorns grew up and choked it, and it yielded no grain. Other seed fell into good soil and brought forth grain, growing up and increasing and yielding thirty and sixty and a hundredfold." And he said, "Let anyone with ears to hear listen!"

Consider This

The Holy Spirit works through Jesus to communicate the nature of God and the gospel in a variety of ways. Last week the analogy was fishing for people. This week it's sowing the seeds of the gospel into the soil of peoples' lives. As we read through the Bible, we witness a God who longs to communicate with people. He often utilizes something we understand (like seeds) to teach us about something we struggle to grasp (like the nature of God).

The Spirit reveals a God who works like an extravagant sower. The Holy Spirit is long on extravagance and short on efficiency. Efficiency wants to do the research and determine the location of the good soil in advance and only sow there. This is not how the gospel works. The gospel works through abundant extravagant sowing—everywhere and all the time. I mean, who sows seed on the path?

According to this parable, something like three out of every four seeds sown fails. At the same time, no effort to sow the gospel will ever be a failure. Regardless of whether it amounts to anything or not, the simple act of sowing the seed communicates the extravagant love of God. The Spirit of God never stops sowing the seed of the good news of Jesus Christ.

Despite the high fail rate, one seed in four returns an extraordinary harvest. Let's put this in the framework of money. Say I give you one million dollars. According to the parable (and I realize this is not some kind of formula), you will lose $250,000 right off the top—gone! The next $500,000 will seem to be a good investment. The seed will sprout and grow and yet it will ultimately fail and amount to a total loss. This leaves you with $250,000 of the one million. Let's average the yield on that $250,000 to a 60-fold return. That comes to a gain of $15,000,000 if my math is right.

Final thought. The harvest is not up to the sower. The sower's only job is to sow extravagantly . . . everywhere . . . all the time. The pressure's off. The Holy Spirit will bring the return. It comes down to being willing to have a high fail rate while knowing you cannot fail.

In 1923, Babe Ruth broke three major league baseball records. He broke the record for the most home runs in a single season. He broke the record for the highest batting average in a single season. And, most surprisingly, in this same season, he led the entire league in strikeouts.

a Christian will spread the gospel yet only a few will take root, But those will grow in faith and spread more & more gospel —

J. D. WALT

In some ways, I think this may be how the gospel works. It's about a high fail rate without failing.

The Prayer

Spirit of the living God, fall afresh on me.

The Questions

- What will it take to bring you to a greater confidence in the seed of the Word of God?
- What will it take to make you an extravagant sower? What holds you back?

19 Why the Holy Spirit Prefers Curious People

MARK 4:10–20 | When he was alone, the Twelve and the others around him asked him about the parables. He told them, "The secret of the kingdom of God has been given to you. But to those on the outside everything is said in parables so that, 'they may be ever seeing but never perceiving, and ever hearing but never understanding; otherwise they might turn and be forgiven!'"

Then Jesus said to them, "Don't you understand this parable? How then will you understand any parable? The farmer sows the word. Some people are like seed along the path, where the word is sown. As soon as they hear it, Satan comes and takes away the word that was sown in them. Others, like seed sown on rocky places, hear the word and at once receive it with joy. But since they have no root, they last only a short time. When trouble or persecution comes because of the word, they quickly fall away. Still others, like seed sown among thorns, hear the word; but the worries of this life, the deceitfulness of wealth and the desires for other things come in and choke the word, making it unfruitful. Others, like seed sown on good soil, hear the word, accept it, and produce a crop—some thirty, some sixty, some a hundred times what was sown."

Consider This

It has always puzzled me. Why does Jesus seemingly indicate he wants to conceal the meaning of the parables?

But to those on the outside everything is said in parables so that, "they may be ever seeing but never perceiving, and ever hearing but never understanding; otherwise they might turn and be forgiven!"

I have a working theory on this. Parables serve as a kind of fishing technique for Jesus. He casts a large net. A certain number of people find themselves caught up in the puzzle of the parable enough to pursue its meaning. Those who ask Jesus for explanation or clarification are the ones to whom the meaning is given.

When he was alone, the Twelve and the others around him asked him about the parables.

I suspect if they had not asked Jesus about the parables, he may not have explained them. What if the key to receiving the secrets of the kingdom of God is simply asking Jesus? Could it be that simple? The passage from seeing to perceiving and from hearing to understanding is humble curiosity—the courage to ask.

Why won't people just ask? Could it be we don't want to reveal our own ignorance? Could it be we think we already have it figured out? Could it be we don't want to ask for help because we think we are smart enough to figure it out on our own? What do each of these scenarios have in common? The answer is pride.

The Holy Spirit can't do much with a prideful person. Prideful people tend to have a low teachability quotient. Could it be that parables tuck the wisdom and insight beneath the surface, out of the reach of those who would readily convert the knowledge into more power for themselves. The kingdom of God will not be manipulated into any empire's establishment. The knowledge and wisdom of God's kingdom is revealed only to the humble. Could it be that a person's receptivity to the Holy Spirit is equal to their humility?

It makes sense. After all, why didn't Jesus choose the religious leaders and teachers of the Law to become his disciples? Probably because they already knew it all. Teachers often surprisingly turn out to be the least teachable people of all. The best teachers, however, turnout to be the most teachable people. No matter how much they learn, they keep risking the humility of curiosity. Asking questions requires one to publicly admit they don't have all the answers.

Sometimes I can sit in front of a biblical text for what seems like forever, trying to figure out its meaning or develop some kind of creative angle of teaching. The harder I try, the more opaque the text can seem to me. Finally, the aha moment comes, but it's not the aha of finding the meaning. It's the aha of humility; giving up on my skills and submitting to asking Jesus to show me the meaning. He always does. I find the more I think I know about something, the less curious I am and the less I am able to learn anything new.

So how about you? Are you a curious person? Willing to ask questions? Let's work together to become curious before the text, ready to ask Jesus at the beginning of our exploration rather than as a last resort. And let's learn to approach others like that too.

The Prayer
Spirit of the living God, fall afresh on me.

The Questions
- What is your teachability quotient?
- Do you tend to be curious before God's Word or to think you already know what it means?

20 Not for Ourselves but Others: The Great Rule of the Kingdom

MARK 4:21–25 ESV | And he said to them, "Is a lamp brought in to be put under a basket, or under a bed, and not on a stand? For nothing is hidden except to be made manifest; nor is anything secret except to come to light. If anyone has ears to hear, let him hear." And he said to them, "Pay attention to what you hear: with the measure you use, it will be measured to you, and still more will be added to you. For to the one who has, more will be given, and from the one who has not, even what he has will be taken away."

Consider This

Just as many of you read the Daily Text faithfully each week, I also have certain writings I read to encourage my growth in the grace of God. Every morning I read the daily writings of Dr. Gary Hoag, a.k.a. "The Generosity Monk," a close friend and co-laborer in the work of the gospel. Just recently he posted a quote I think powerfully captures the ideas at work in today's text. The quote comes from Edward Payson:

"Not for ourselves, but others"—is the grand law of nature, inscribed by the hand of God on every part of creation. Not for itself, but others, does the sun dispense its beams; not for themselves, but others, do the clouds distil their showers; not for herself, but others, does the earth unlock her treasures; not for themselves, but others, do the trees produce their fruits, or the flowers diffuse their fragrance and display their various hues. So, not for himself, but others, are the blessings of Heaven bestowed on man; and whenever, instead of diffusing them around, he devotes them exclusively to his own gratification, and shuts himself up in the dark and flinty caverns of selfishness, he transgresses the great law of creation—he cuts himself off from the created universe, and its Author—he sacrilegiously converts to his own use the favors which were given him for the relief of others, and must be considered, not only as an unprofitable, but as a fraudulent servant, who has worse than wasted his Lord's money. He, who thus lives only to himself, and consumes the bounty of Heaven upon his lusts, or consecrates it to the demon of avarice, is a barren rock in a fertile plain; he is a thorny bramble in a fruitful vineyard; he is the grave of God's blessings.[1]

Gary comes up with this kind of gold almost every single day. Because this particular reading spoke powerfully to me concerning today's text and because I also want to be faithful to "put the lamp on the stand," I wanted to share his work

---

1. Edward Payson (1783–1827) American Congregationalist preacher in *Selections from the Conversations and Unpublished Writings of Rev. Edward Payson*, excerpt from "Universal Law of Benevolence" (Boston: Crocker & Brewster, 1836), 171.

with you and encourage you to follow Gary at his website generositymonk.com.

The Prayer

Spirit of the living God, fall afresh on me.

The Questions

- Have you found all the ways you can serve others but still be serving yourself? Explain.

21 A Parable about the Most Humble Power in the World

MARK 4:26–34 NRSV | He also said, "The kingdom of God is as if someone would scatter seed on the ground, and would sleep and rise night and day, and the seed would sprout and grow, he does not know how. The earth produces of itself, first the stalk, then the head, then the full grain in the head. But when the grain is ripe, at once he goes in with his sickle, because the harvest has come."

He also said, "With what can we compare the kingdom of God, or what parable will we use for it? It is like a mustard seed, which, when sown upon the ground, is the smallest of all the seeds on earth; yet when it is sown it grows up and becomes the greatest of all shrubs, and puts forth large branches, so that the birds of the air can make nests in its shade."

With many such parables he spoke the word to them, as they were able to hear it; he did not speak to them except in parables, but he explained everything in private to his disciples.

Consider This

Do you remember the last time you looked at a seed? It's something so common we scarcely pay any attention to it at all. How could something so small hold so much potential?

When Jesus reaches for a way to teach us about the kingdom of God, he reaches for a seed. He could reach for the tree or the fruit that grows on the tree, but instead he chooses the seed to make his point.

Consider a single apple seed. This seed contains all the compounded possibilities of the entire tree. Every branch and leaf and future apple is contained in the one tiny singular seed. Residing in this one seed are all the trees that will come in the future from the seeds produced by this one seed. I once heard this African proverb, "Anyone can tell you how many seeds are in an apple, but only God knows how many apples are in a seed."

Maybe I'm stating the obvious, and perhaps that's the point. It's so easy to miss the mystery because it is obscured by the ordinary. Maybe this is why Jesus is constantly calling forth eyes that see and ears that hear. The truth is shining like a candle on a lamp stand, yet somehow we can miss seeing it entirely. The kingdom is not meant to be hidden, but revealed, yet it takes a certain kind of seeing to perceive it.

What could be more humble than a tiny seed, yet what could be more grand than the tallest tree? This is what God's kingdom is like—on earth yet from heaven. In fact, this is what Jesus is like—full of humanity and full of the Holy Spirit.

Parables cannot be pinned down, only pondered. They cannot be forced into our categories and systems. They cause us to humble ourselves before a wisdom we would not otherwise discover. A parable leads the curious seeker into the realm of divine revelation. It takes the learner out of control of the knowledge. Parables put everyone on equal footing, stripping away the prestigious academic robes of distinction, withholding understanding from the proud and revealing it to little children.

Jesus, the text says, never taught them anything without using a parable. Why is it that we so prize our systematic approaches that try to teach everything without them? Parables bring disciples into a different relationship with learning. They take away from us our penchant to master the material and lead us to the place where we are mastered by the Messiah.

A closing thought on seeds from the parables in today's text: all we do is sow the seed. The seed does everything else. Yet if we do not sow it, it does nothing. That is a massively powerful, obvious, yet hidden truth. How do you like them apples?

The Prayer

Spirit of the living God, fall afresh on me.

The Questions

- What are your reflections on the potential and power of a seed?
- How might you look upon your life in such ways?

Who Needs the Weather Channel When You've Got Jesus?

22

MARK 4:35–41 | That day when evening came, he said to his disciples, "Let us go over to the other side." Leaving the crowd behind, they took him along, just as he was, in the boat. There were also other boats with him. A furious squall came up, and the waves broke over the boat, so that it was nearly swamped. Jesus was in the stern, sleeping on a cushion. The disciples woke him and said to him, "Teacher, don't you care if we drown?"

He got up, rebuked the wind and said to the waves, "Quiet! Be still!" Then the wind died down and it was completely calm.

He said to his disciples, "Why are you so afraid? Do you still have no faith?"

They were terrified and asked each other, "Who is this? Even the wind and the waves obey him!"

Consider This

Who does that? He doesn't run for cover (as though that could be done in a boat). He speaks to the storm. In fact, he speaks to the storm in the same way he will soon be speaking to demons—sternly.

Quiet! Be still!

I remember a few years back I was part of a weekend outdoor gathering of college students in North Texas, a solemn assembly. On the first night of the gathering, a massive storm blew in; in the tradition of, *"A furious squall came up, and the waves broke over the boat, so that it was nearly swamped."*

I was charged with pastoral leadership of the team of speakers and worship leaders who would lead the gathering. Did I mention there were about thirty thousand college students camping in tents? That would be the next worst thing to being in a boat in the midst of such a storm. Lightning was popping all around us. We were frantic. I gathered the leaders close and reminded them of Jesus calming the storm and urged us to go for it. And we did. I've never spoken so sternly to a storm before or since. To my and the group's chagrin, the storm only worsened. In fact, a couple of kids were struck by lightning that night yet their lives were miraculously spared. Bottom line: we failed miserably in our role as storm-stillers.

In response to Jesus' three-word command we get this response: *"Then the wind died down and it was completely calm."*

So what's the big difference in these two scenarios (besides the fact that Jesus is God and we were not)? You know by now that I am convinced that as it was with Jesus so it is with his followers. I do believe it is possible for a human being filled with the Holy Spirit to take authority, even over the weather and command it to cease. Okay, I've never seen it happen, but I still hold out the possibility.

Upon further reflection on this story, I have another insight I'll run by you. For my money, the big miracle that night was not that Jesus stilled the storm. The big miracle was that Jesus remained unflinchingly still in the midst of the storm. It's actually better than that. In the face of a furious and obviously life-threatening storm, Mark gives us this tidbit: *Jesus was in the stern, sleeping on a cushion.*

Looking back on that stormy night in Texas, one of the big differences between our group and Jesus was that we were absolutely frantic. Jesus was unphased by the storm, so much so that he could have slept right through it. That my friends, is what they call, "peace like a river."

What if it's our quality of peace within the storm that determines the capacity of our faith to calm the storm? If I'm honest, in the face of life's many storms, I'm typically not napping. I'm doing my best to keep the lid on my anxiety.

Maybe that's why the Holy Spirit inspired Paul to instruct us, "Do not be anxious about anything, but in every situation, by prayer and petition, with thanksgiving . . ." (Phil. 4:6).

Peace is a fruit of the Holy Spirit. The Holy Spirit was Jesus' peace, not only beyond understanding but beyond measure. He will do the same in us.

We may never enjoy the opportunity to calm a hurricane, but in the midst of a furious squall like cancer or divorce or some other tragic circumstance, we may find it's the Holy Spirit empowered stillness of our spirit that calms the winds and raises the faith of everyone in the boat around us.

I know people like that. You do too. Let's become one of them. Fix in your mind's eye the image of Jesus sleeping in the midst of that furious squall. Ask the Holy Spirit to raise your faith to the level of that possibility.

The Prayer
Spirit of the living God, fall afresh on me.

The Questions
- What do you think lies behind the anxiety in your life? What is its source?
- What might it look like to start dealing with it at a new level?

On Becoming the Kind of People Who Don't Give up on People

23

MARK 5:1–8 ESV | They came to the other side of the sea, to the country of the Gerasenes. And when Jesus had stepped out of the boat, immediately there met him out of the tombs a man with an unclean spirit. He lived among the tombs. And no one could bind him anymore, not even with a chain, for he had often been bound with shackles and chains, but he wrenched the chains apart, and he broke the shackles in pieces. No one had the strength to subdue him. Night and day among the tombs and on the mountains he was always crying out and cutting himself with stones. And when he saw Jesus from afar, he ran and fell down before him. And crying out with a loud voice, he said, "What have you to do with me, Jesus, Son of the Most High God? I adjure you by God, do not torment me." For he was saying to him, "Come out of the man, you unclean spirit!"

Consider This

We are moving into a series of stories that I would label as "impossible situations." Today we see a man possessed by a demonic presence. The demons had literally driven him insane. They drove him into an exilic place of death: a grave yard. How much further from life and light could a person go? This was a person who had been written off, discarded, and left completely alone. Not only could he not be helped, he could not be restrained. He was completely disconnected from people and was totally at odds with himself, cutting himself with stones. We are looking at an extreme case, an impossible situation. How will Jesus respond to him?

Here's what I find most interesting about this part of the story. The demonic spirits drove this man to the most isolated place on earth. This is the gravity of darkness and death. With the entrance of the presence of God, the gravity of the Holy Spirit overwhelmed the gravity of the evil spirits and literally pulled this man to the very feet of Jesus. No one could restrain this man, yet the Spirit of God seemed to move him almost effortlessly to the feet of Jesus.

The Holy Spirit, through the person of Jesus, and now through the body of Christ, walks right into the midst of the darkest places, into the most impossible situations and hopeless causes and sets captives free. The Holy Spirit, who is in you, is infinitely more powerful than the evil spirits who are in the world. The Holy Spirit never gives up on people, no matter what. When the Holy Spirit has full reign in us, he makes us the kind of people who never give up on people, no matter what.

The question we must answer is, Do we want to become the kind of people who never give up on people, who will believe beyond belief in the possibilities of God for anyone and everyone? These are the kind of people the Holy Spirit searches to find. To become this kind of person requires a willful decision on our part. It will mean being transformed into the shape of the love of God. We aren't responsible to solve the problem. We are responsible to show up, to be present to Jesus in the presence of people facing impossible situations, and to be ever saying, sometimes aloud and other times under our breath, "Come Holy Spirit!"

The Prayer

Spirit of the living God, fall afresh on me.

The Questions

- Ask the Spirit to bring to mind impossible situations in your own life or in the lives of others in your sphere. Write those down.
- How are you dealing with the impossible situations? Giving up? Grasping for more love?
- Could these situations be a test to see if you will give up?

Do You Believe in Demons?

24

MARK 5:9–20 NRSV | Then Jesus asked him, "What is your name?" He replied, "My name is Legion; for we are many." He begged him earnestly not to send them out of the country. Now there on the hillside a great herd of swine was feeding; and the unclean spirits begged him, "Send us into the swine;

let us enter them." So he gave them permission. And the unclean spirits came out and entered the swine; and the herd, numbering about two thousand, rushed down the steep bank into the sea, and were drowned in the sea.

The swineherds ran off and told it in the city and in the country. Then people came to see what it was that had happened. They came to Jesus and saw the demoniac sitting there, clothed and in his right mind, the very man who had had the legion; and they were afraid. Those who had seen what had happened to the demoniac and to the swine reported it. Then they began to beg Jesus to leave their neighborhood. As he was getting into the boat, the man who had been possessed by demons begged him that he might be with him. But Jesus refused, and said to him, "Go home to your friends, and tell them how much the Lord has done for you, and what mercy he has shown you." And he went away and began to proclaim in the Decapolis how much Jesus had done for him; and everyone was amazed.

Consider This

When you have a quantity of demonic spirits with capability to possess a herd of two thousand pigs and they are all living in the same person, you have an impossible situation. But if there's one thing we know from reading the Bible, it's that nothing is impossible with God.

Jesus specializes in chaos. He walks right into the jaws of chaos and brings forth order. He did it earlier in the deadly storm on the Sea of Galilee. In today's text, he takes on the chaos of unimaginable demonic possession. Imagine the storm on the Sea of Galilee with all its chaos raging inside of a single human being. That's what he's facing.

Before we go further into this Gospel, we need to ask ourselves a couple of questions. We need to take a bit of a reality check. First, do we hold to a biblical view of the world with categories for visible and invisible? Seen and unseen? How about natural and supernatural? What about demonic beings and angelic beings? The Bible does not set out to prove these dimensions of reality. It assumes them. Given the scientific age in which we live, many are dismissive of the biblical worldview as a relic of pre-modern times. I am not one of those people. I have neither an overly simplistic nor a highly sophisticated understanding of the categories inherent in a biblical worldview. That said, believing in an unseen reality strikes me as a fundamental requirement of faith and a prerequisite for biblical Christianity.

I trust in the veracity and the authority of the Bible. When Scripture speaks of the Holy Spirit, I believe it. When Scripture speaks of demonic beings, I believe it. When Scripture speaks of angelic visitations, I believe it. While my understanding of such realities continues to grow, my faith in the biblical revelation of the nature of reality; past, present, and future; visible and invisible remains as fixed as the sun. This is not blind, easy, believism. It is the hard-fought, time-tested fruit of faith. Many God-fearing Christians remain agnostic on these matters, content to live out their lives with the conviction of a hung jury. While I don't want to insist on belief in demonic spirits as essential to saving faith, I do believe that robust growth in the Christian faith requires one to lean trustingly into the biblical worldview rather than accepting the easy agnosticism of our age.

Here are the basic contours of my own developing theology of the demonic, all of which I see at work in today's text. First, demonic presence distorts human identity. Second, apart from the indwelling presence and power of the Holy Spirit, human beings are defenseless against demonic forces. Third, the reign of Jesus (a.k.a., the kingdom of God) means the present power of the Holy Spirit to provide protection from and aid to prevail decisively over demonic forces (i.e., "Deliver us from evil").

I am an appreciator of C. S. Lewis's piercingly pragmatic take on Satan and demons in his classic book, *The Screwtape Letters*. Because I need to close, I'll limit my references to two favorite quotes of the senior demon to Wormwood, the apprentice.

This first quote references the unintelligent lack of belief in the demonic by so many:

My Dear Wormwood,

I wonder you should ask me whether it is essential to keep the patient in ignorance of your own existence. That question, at least for the present phase of the struggle, has been answered for us by the High Command. Our policy, for the moment, is to conceal ourselves. . . . I do not think you will have much difficulty in keeping the patient in the dark. The fact that "devils" are predominantly *comic* figures in the modern imagination will help you. If any faint suspicion of your existence begins to arise in his mind, suggest to him a picture of something in red tights, and persuade him that since he cannot believe in that (it is an old text-book method of confusing them) he therefore cannot believe in you.[2]

The second quote references the uninformed lack of faith in the power of Jesus and his church.

One of our great allies at present is the Church itself. Do not misunderstand me. I do not mean the Church as we see her spread but through all time and space and rooted in eternity, terrible as an army with banners. That, I confess, is a spectacle which makes our boldest tempters uneasy. But fortunately it is quite invisible to these humans.[3]

The Prayer
Spirit of the living God, fall afresh on me.

The Questions
- Where are you in your understanding and belief in the reality of evil, Satan, and demons?
- Can you afford to be agnostic about it?

---

2. C. S. Lewis, *The Screwtape Letters* (New York: HarperCollins, 2001), 31–32.

3. Lewis, *Screwtape Letters*, 5.

25 | The Problem of Reducing People to Their Problems

MARK 5:21–29 | When Jesus had again crossed over by boat to the other side of the lake, a large crowd gathered around him while he was by the lake. Then one of the synagogue leaders, named Jairus, came, and when he saw Jesus, he fell at his feet. He pleaded earnestly with him, "My little daughter is dying. Please come and put your hands on her so that she will be healed and live." So Jesus went with him.

A large crowd followed and pressed around him. And a woman was there who had been subject to bleeding for twelve years. She had suffered a great deal under the care of many doctors and had spent all she had, yet instead of getting better she grew worse. When she heard about Jesus, she came up behind him in the crowd and touched his cloak, because she thought, "If I just touch his clothes, I will be healed." Immediately her bleeding stopped and she felt in her body that she was freed from her suffering.

Consider This

Did you catch what just happened? Jesus is now back on the other side of the lake. It turns out he went to the region of the Gerasenes for the sole purpose of delivering the demon-possessed man from evil. That was it.

It's Father's Day as I'm writing this. As I reflect on this story, something new strikes me about the ministry of Jesus. I have only ever thought of the demon-possessed man as "the demoniac," or "the man among the tombs." I saw him as the sum total of his problem. Consequently, I saw Jesus as his solution, or his Savior.

While that's undeniable, there's something much bigger going on here. Jesus didn't see this man as "the demoniac." He didn't classify him according to his problem. Jesus saw him as someone's son. No one planned for his life to turn out this way, living in bondage to satanic enslavement. Imagine the heartbreak of his mother and father; a son who was for all practical purposes dead, yet endlessly suffering in agony.

The mission of Jesus, the Son of God, sent by the Father, is the restoration of all sons and daughters. His was and remains on a mission to reclaim and restore what has been lost; the sons of Adam and the daughters of Eve. At the heart of the heart of God beats the love of a Father.

Learning to see people as God sees them means I can never label them according to their suffering. I must see them as sons and daughters. Everyone on earth is someone's son or daughter. What if we could see them like that?

The theme continues in today's text with the leader of the synagogue—also a father.

"My little daughter is dying. Please come and put your hands on her so that she will be healed and live."

Jesus likely needed little convincing as the little girl was only twelve years old. As they turned toward this bleak scenario, yet another impossible situation presented itself. We will pick up with that one tomorrow.

The Prayer

Spirit of the living God, fall afresh on me.

The Questions

- Do you tend to see people in need as the sum total of their problems, especially people in need that you do not know (i.e., the poor)?
- What if we saw them as God sees them?

26 A Word for Women (and Men) That Can Change Everything

MARK 5:30–36 ESV | And Jesus, perceiving in himself that power had gone out from him, immediately turned about in the crowd and said, "Who touched my garments?" And his disciples said to him, "You see the crowd pressing around you, and yet you say, 'Who touched me?'" And he looked around to see who had done it. But the woman, knowing what had happened to her, came in fear and trembling and fell down before him and told him the whole truth. And he said to her, "Daughter, your faith has made you well; go in peace, and be healed of your disease."

While he was still speaking, there came from the ruler's house some who said, "Your daughter is dead. Why trouble the Teacher any further?" But overhearing what they said, Jesus said to the ruler of the synagogue, "Do not fear, only believe."

Consider This

Remember, Jesus didn't see people as the sum of their problems but rather as the sons and daughters of the Father. Today's text provides us another great example. If I'm honest, I've always labeled this woman who had been bleeding for twelve years and who was trying to reach out and touch Jesus to be healed as just that, a sick woman who had suffered greatly and spent all her money on doctors who couldn't heal her. I summed her up according to her problems.

She did, in fact, manage to find her way through the pressing crowd to reach out and touch his clothes. Instantly, she was healed. Now here's the fascinating part. How is it that Jesus could, on the one hand, know that power had gone out from him (a major phenomenon in itself) and, on the other hand, not know where the power went. His disciples went in the other direction, asking how on earth he could possibly know who touched him with all these people crowding around him. For my money, Jesus knew exactly who touched him. I mean, anyone who has the supernatural sensitivity to know that power had gone out from him knows where it went, right?

This was a setup. *And he looked around to see who had done it.* He was on an urgent mission to the home of a little girl who was at death's door. Why did it matter so much to Jesus to know? Here's my theory and I think the text bears it out.

Jesus knew who she was and he wanted her to identify herself because a much deeper and richer and even more powerful healing was needed. *But the woman, knowing what had happened to her, came in fear and trembling and fell down before him and told him the whole truth.* Here's a woman who, from the get-go, was like every other woman in the first century, a person without status. Beyond that, she was perpetually unclean because of her bleeding, which kept her from being able to relate like even a normal woman in the community. She was a very, very marginal person in the world. Beyond that, she was interrupting a Rabbi (a.k.a., Jesus) who was en route to help a man of high status, Jairus the synagogue leader, on a desperate 9-1-1 mission. Is it any wonder she fell at his feet and, trembling with fear, told him the whole truth?

I am convinced this was a setup to create this unprecedented opportunity for Jesus, the Son of God, to speak the gospel to her in a single word: *daughter*. Of all the things she likely thought of herself—like how she probably deserved this plague of a condition for something she had done somewhere in her past, or how ashamed her family must be of her for all these years, or how she might rather just disappear and die than be exposed publicly like this—she wasn't likely thinking of herself as the beloved daughter of a loving father. Daughter. There are a lot of women reading this who need to hear this word spoken into the depths of your being: *daughter*. You are the beloved daughter of a perfect Father who sees beyond the shame you may have suffered. You are the beloved daughter of a divine Father who can hold you and speak into you and heal you from all the brokenness that may have been caused by your own broken earthly father. Daughter.

And he said to her, "Daughter, your faith has made you well; go in peace, and be healed of your disease."

Two days ago it was a son being freed from his suffering. Today we behold freedom for a beloved daughter. I think there's also a word tucked in here for those of us who are fathers if we're listening.

The good news: one daughter is healed. The bad news: another daughter is dead.

While he was still speaking, there came from the ruler's house some who said, "Your daughter is dead. Why trouble the Teacher any further?" But overhearing what they said, Jesus said to the ruler of the synagogue, "Do not fear, only believe."

The worst four words a parent could hear: "Your daughter is dead." Jesus counters with the five most hopeful words: *"Do not fear, only believe."*

God is not only better than we think, he's better than we can possibly imagine.

Most days, many of us have occasion and opportunity to speak these words to someone who needs to hear them. Commit those five words to memory and ask the Spirit to bring them to mind when needed.

The Prayer

Spirit of the living God, fall afresh on me.

The Questions

- Which is the deeper healing here—the healing of her sickness or the healing of her identity? How might these two things have been related?
- Do you see any parallels in your life and community today? How does your identity need deep healing?

27 Up, Girl!

MARK 5:37–43 NRSV | He allowed no one to follow him except Peter, James, and John, the brother of James. When they came to the house of the leader of the synagogue, he saw a commotion, people weeping and wailing loudly. When he had entered, he said to them, "Why do you make a commotion and weep? The child is not dead but sleeping." And they laughed at him. Then he put them all outside, and took the child's father and mother and those who were with him, and went in where the child was. He took her by the hand and said to her, "Talitha cum," which means, "Little girl, get up!" And immediately the girl got up and began to walk about (she was twelve years of age). At this they were overcome with amazement. He strictly ordered them that no one should know this, and told them to give her something to eat

Consider This

When it comes to the work of the Holy Spirit on earth, faith is the coin of the realm. Notice Jesus only took a very select group of people with him into the home where the little girl lay dead. He took her parents, Peter, James, and John. He took the inner circle. Why? He could have gone in alone and taken care of it. The girl was dead. Jesus goes in alone. He comes out carrying her and presents her to her parents. That's a good story. Jesus gets all the credit and all the glory, right?

So why the entourage? For starters, we must remember Jesus is always making disciples for the transformation of the world. This is a prime disciple-making moment. Then and now, Jesus wants his disciples to have a full repertoire of ministry experiences. Healing? Check. Prophetic speech? Check. Setting captives free from demonic strongholds? Check. Raising a little girl from the dead? Check!

We need to grasp that just as the first disciples had these profound experiences in their memory, so we have them in ours. Faith means living out of the memory of the past performance of Jesus.

Second, I think that's why Jesus took these particular people into the house. They had faith. Jairus would never have left his home in such a crisis to go and find Jesus miles away had he no faith in him. These three disciples had seen him perform miracle after miracle. They had faith. Additionally, these disciples had a deep hope. And God knows those parents were hoping against hope for a miracle. Recall in the end only three things last forever: faith, hope, and, yes, love.

And which is the greatest? BINGO—love! I began by saying faith was the coin of the realm in the kingdom of God. I stand corrected. Love is the coin of the realm. The only person who loved this little girl more than her parents was Jesus, and Jesus was teaching his faith-filled disciples what the love of God looks like and how it works. As Paul wrote to the Galatians, "The only thing that counts is faith expressing itself through love" (Gal. 5:6).

Faith is a go-for-it mentality, but lest faith be steeped in hope and trained by love it will not work. Love never fails. Miracle or no miracle, love never fails.

I keep remembering that storm on the Sea of Galilee, the near-death experience. Could it be that Jesus allowed these disciples to endure a near-death experience so they might be more attuned to the near-death experiences happening all around them all the time? Faith moving in love looks like the Holy Spirit bringing the overwhelming calm of peace right into the eye of the storm. Did you pick up the detail about the scene? The text described it as *"a commotion, with people crying and wailing loudly."* This was Level 1 Trauma.

That storm on the Sea of Galilee . . . it never stopped. Though the winds were calmed, the storm never stopped. The storm raged among the tombs as the demon-possessed man wandered in pain. The storm raged twelve years in the life of the woman who could not find a cure. The storm raged in the home of Jairus as his daughter lay dead. The storm raged right up to the cross itself and beyond. And it rages to the present day. The storm will not prevail but it will not stop until the very end, until all is said and done. The big deal is not the storm outside, but the peace inside.

It's why Paul tells us, "Do not be anxious about anything, but in every situation, by prayer and petition, with thanksgiving, present your requests to God. And the peace of God, which transcends all understanding, will guard your hearts and your minds in Christ Jesus" (Phil. 4:6–7). The peace of God rules like a sentry standing guard, watching over our hearts and minds, keeping them hidden in the refuge of who Jesus is.

Note the way Jesus speaks simple words in the power of the Spirit in these situations. *Talitha cum!* It means, "Up, Girl!" He says to the storm, "Be still!" He says to lepers, "Be clean!" He says to the blind, "Receive your sight." He says to the paralyzed man, "Arise and go." He says to the parents, "Do not be afraid; only believe." He says to the woman, "Daughter."

To minister in the way of Jesus means we share in his authority to speak such words of power and blessing into the lives of others. What if our words only have effect to the degree they are anchored in the power of his love?

What word of bold love might he be saying to you and me? What word might he have for us to speak into another?

The Prayer

Spirit of the living God, fall afresh on me.

The mind of Christ —Deposit of God—
J. D. WALT Trinity assurance of being
His.

The Questions

- Do you tend to get through your storms by gutting it out or gritting your teeth? Trying to escape them?
- Are you learning to be desperate and needy and vulnerable before Jesus and others?

28 The Kind of Places Where Miracles Don't Happen

MARK 6:1–6 | Jesus left there and went to his hometown, accompanied by his disciples. When the Sabbath came, he began to teach in the synagogue, and many who heard him were amazed.

"Where did this man get these things?" they asked. "What's this wisdom that has been given him? What are these remarkable miracles he is performing? Isn't this the carpenter? Isn't this Mary's son and the brother of James, Joseph, Judas and Simon? Aren't his sisters here with us?" And they took offense at him.

Jesus said to them, "A prophet is not without honor except in his own town, among his relatives and in his own home." He could not do any miracles there, except lay his hands on a few sick people and heal them. He was amazed at their lack of faith.

Consider This

As far as I'm concerned, Mark 6:5 may be the most under-explored text in the whole Gospel.

He could not do any miracles there, except lay his hands on a few sick people and heal them. He was amazed at their lack of faith.

Seriously? He could not do any miracles there? We are talking about one in whom the Holy Spirit dwelled without measure. This is the Son of God, the second person of the Trinity, the Lion of Judah, the Lamb of God who takes away the sins of the world, the Alpha and Omega, the Way and the Truth and the Life, and we could go on.

He could not do any miracles there . . .

Seriously? Did he just not want to do any miracles in his hometown or could he not do any miracles there? How can we say God could not do something? Okay, so we aren't saying that. The Bible is saying it. I do take comfort in the fact that we aren't given a story of Jesus trying to do a miracle and coming up empty. How are we to understand this? We need to look at the end of verse 6.

He was amazed at their lack of faith.

So what does our faith have to do with Jesus' ability to perform or not perform miracles? Apparently, faith has a lot to do with it. So how is this different from the idea of faith-healing, which we typically associate with fraudulent televangelists? What about when a person is not healed and they are told they weren't healed because they didn't have enough faith? What are we to make of that? I think it's an abusive way to respond to a person who did not get healed. What if the little girl had not come back to life at the command of Jesus? Imagine people blaming her for her lack of faith! At the same time, if we believe the Bible, we can't get around the clear connection between faith and miracles.

We are told two things: Jesus could not do miracles there, and he was amazed at their lack of faith.

So what if miracles are a social phenomenon. What if they require a certain kind of community in order to happen? It gets us away from connecting miracles to the faith of the individual person in need of a miracle; though Scripture is also clear that an individual's faith plays a role in the process. Jesus told the hemorrhaging woman that her faith had made her well. Jesus only took those parents and the three insider disciples into the home of the dead little girl. Faith had something to do with that.

Where does this leave us? First, we need to understand that miracles are a sovereign act of the love of God. Faith does not make miracles happen. God makes miracles happen. However, there are places where miracles tend to happen and places where they do not tend to happen. What's the difference? God is the same regardless of place. I think we've resolved that it does not come down to the faith of an individual person.

I will forever remember a marquee sign I saw several years ago, on a bank of all places. The sign said, "Where there is great love, miracles always happen." I think the issue is love, or the

THE GOSPEL OF THE HOLY SPIRIT

lack thereof. The power of God sovereignly works miracles in response to the faith of a community moving in love.

Could it be we don't see miracles too much these days because of the anemic levels of biblical faith in our communities? By biblical faith, I mean faith anchored not in the love of power but in the power of love. I've been in a lot of situations where people of faith wanted to see a demonstration of power and it didn't happen. I think the Holy Spirit is in search of communities who long to see a demonstration of holy love. Where there is great love, miracles always happen.

The Prayer

Spirit of the living God, fall afresh on me.

The Questions

- What if the real issue behind anemic faith is actually broken love? Wouldn't we want to open ourselves up to the Great Physician for healing of that brokenness?

When people struggle with broken marriage loss of job etc. They Are beaten down.

It Takes Two to Bring the Kingdom

29

MARK 6:6–13 ESV | And he marveled because of their unbelief.

And he went about among the villages teaching.

And he called the twelve and began to send them out two by two, and gave them authority over the unclean spirits. He charged them to take nothing for their journey except a staff—no bread, no bag, no money in their belts—but to wear sandals and not put on two tunics. And he said to them, "Whenever you enter a house, stay there until you depart from there. And if any place will not receive you and they will not listen to you, when you leave, shake off the dust that is on your feet as a testimony against them." So they went out and proclaimed that people should repent. And they cast out many demons and anointed with oil many who were sick and healed them.

Consider This

And he went about among the villages teaching. Never underestimate the significance of the ministry of teaching. There is no substitute for it. Teaching paves the way for the in-breaking kingdom of God. Preaching opens the door. Deliverance and healing demonstrate the kingdom's arrival.

And he called the twelve and began to send them out two by two,

Why two by two? It seems like they could have covered twice as much ground if each had been sent to a different place? Remember, the kingdom of God is not about the efficiency of labor but the extravagance of holy love. My theory on why he sent them two by two? The Holy Spirit prefers to work through relationships over individuals. Jesus taught on another occasion that where two or three gather in his name he is there among them. He also told his disciples that people would know them as his followers by the way they loved each other. He sent them out two by two intending their relationships to be seedbeds—demonstration plots for the kingdom of God. We tend to think God works primarily through individual people. I don't think so. The Bible indicates God's best work happens in and through relationships. Think about it this way. Nothing happens in the kingdom of God apart from the interrelationships among the Father and the Son and the Holy Spirit. As it is in the Trinity, so it will be in the community of God's people. On earth as it is in heaven . . . right?

Think through how the various relationships and small communities across your own life's landscape can become consecrated to God for his purposes in the world. Ask God to demonstrate his kingdom in and through your relationships.

. . . *and gave them authority over the unclean spirits.* This is a far larger miracle in and of itself than we can imagine. A mere fallen human being is capable of carrying the authority of Jesus, the one in whom the Spirit dwells beyond measure, the Son of God, the second person of the Trinity. Jesus' authority can be transferred. This is astonishing. There is no higher authority than the authority of Jesus and he entrusts it to his followers. Are you in touch with this possibility in your own life? Isn't this the whole point of discipleship: to learn from Jesus how to live under and through his authority, which is to live in the fullness of his Spirit for the sake of blessing others?

Take nothing for [the] journey. This kind of flies in the face of the good old Boy Scout motto, doesn't it? "Be prepared." Or what if Jesus is merely changing the nature of what it means to be prepared. What if being prepared does not mean trying to anticipate every possible scenario that could happen? What if being prepared means to live in complete trust and dependence on the presence, power, and provision of God? That sounds about right to me. It doesn't seem reasonable or practical. While I think this is the ideal of the kingdom life, I don't think it is the non-negotiable requirement. Life in the kingdom of God strikes me as a risk-reward scenario. The greater the risk we are willing to take, the greater the reward. After all, after Jesus, only Peter can claim to have walked on water.

What if that's also part of the two by two dynamic? Learning interdependence. It's a massive challenge in the land of independent rugged individualism.

Today's text gives us a clear window into the unconventionality of Jesus' teaching. It seems unreasonable. But what if our idea of reasonable is unreasonable? Could that be possible?

The Prayer
Spirit of the living God, fall afresh on me.

The Questions
- How do you relate to the instruction from Jesus to take nothing for the journey?
- Are you an always prepared kind of person? How might Jesus want to change our idea of what being prepared means?

The End of Christian America

30

MARK 6:14-20 NRSV | King Herod heard of it, for Jesus' name had become known. Some were saying, "John the baptizer has been raised from the dead; and for this reason these powers are at work in him." But others said, "It is Elijah." And others said, "It is a prophet, like one of the prophets of old." But when Herod heard of it, he said, "John, whom I beheaded, has been raised."

For Herod himself had sent men who arrested John, bound him, and put him in prison on account of Herodias, his brother Philip's wife, because Herod had married her. For John had been telling Herod, "It is not lawful for you to have your brother's wife." And Herodias had a grudge against him, and wanted to kill him. But she could not, for Herod feared John, knowing that he was a righteous and holy man, and he protected him. When he heard him, he was greatly perplexed; and yet he liked to listen to him.

Consider This

There are only two stories. There is the story of the kingdom of God and the story of the world. In the story of the kingdom of God, Jesus is everything and the only thing. In the story of the world, Jesus is many things and he is nothing.

So far, Mark has pretty much given us the story of the kingdom of God. You remember how Mark began with John the Baptist and by verse 9, he's introducing Jesus. Speaking of the kingdom story, remember Jesus' first message and manifesto: "The time has come," he said. "The kingdom of God has come near. Repent and believe the good news!" (Mark 1:15).

From there Mark has taken us on a deep dive into the kingdom with Jesus, the King.

At the midpoint of chapter 6, Mark changes gears taking us out of the realm of the kingdom and into the story of the world. When it comes to Jesus, the people are all over the place. Despite his growing following, there seems to be a whole lot of people who are only marginally paying attention. To them, Jesus is a phenomenon. He's a news story, a guru, a political leader, a trouble-maker. This group says one thing and that group says another. King Herod, haunted by his own heinous murder of the great prophet John, hears about Jesus and fears he is John raised from the dead.

The thing we need to keep at the forefront of our mind is until Jesus becomes the center of our devotion, he's just another distraction. When Jesus becomes central in our life, the story of the world recedes into the background. When we seek his kingdom and righteousness, we happily discover how the world was always supposed to work. Until then, faith is something we salute, church is a place we go on Sunday (maybe), and life consists of doing everything in our power to make our own agendas work; building our own little kingdoms and generally justifying whatever seems right in our own eyes.

Over the past one hundred years or so, we've lived through a period of what I would call, "Christian America."

In Christian America, everyone was sort of a Christian. It was hard to tell where the world left off and the church began, so seamless was their relationship. Our money didn't say "Caesar." It claimed we trusted in God. We pledged allegiance to a flag while declaring our nation was "under God." The story of the kingdom of the world as we knew it seemed right down the middle of the fairway of the story of the kingdom of God.

In case you missed the memo, "Christian America" is over. Actually, it's been over for some time now. It's just getting more and more painfully obvious. We now move into an era where we can go in one of three directions: (1) We can do everything in our power to rise up and take back "Christian America"; to try and find our way back to that mythical age when so many saw the kingdom vision and the American dream as two sides of the same coin (i.e., Ten Commandments on the courthouse walls, prayer in schools, and more than just Chick-fil-A closed on Sunday). (2) We can humble ourselves, pledge our allegiance solely to King Jesus, and do everything we possibly can to be the real church in America. We can recognize it's *our* calling to declare and demonstrate the beautifully distinctive kingdom of God rather than delegating it to the government, whose calling is to regulate the story of the world according to the will of the world's people. (3) We can go with the flow, celebrating a freedom with no fences, confusing the lines between liberty and love, and otherwise baptizing the will of the world in the name of God.

Blaise Pascal may have said it best in his unpublished *Penses* when he wrote, "We run heedlessly into the abyss after putting something in front of us to stop us from seeing it."

Well-meaning, good-hearted Christians will go down each of these paths. So which way will you go?

There are three paths here, but only two stories: the story of the kingdom and the story of the world.

The Prayer

Spirit of the living God, fall afresh on me.

The Questions

• How do you assess the three options? Is there a fourth?

31 | Why Marriage Is Not about Marriage and What It Is About

MARK 6:21–29 | Finally the opportune time came. On his birthday Herod gave a banquet for his high officials and military commanders and the leading men of Galilee. When the daughter of Herodias came in and danced, she pleased Herod and his dinner guests.

The king said to the girl, "Ask me for anything you want, and I'll give it to you." And he promised her with an oath, "Whatever you ask I will give you, up to half my kingdom."

She went out and said to her mother, "What shall I ask for?"

"The head of John the Baptist," she answered.

At once the girl hurried in to the king with the request: "I want you to give me right now the head of John the Baptist on a platter."

The king was greatly distressed, but because of his oaths and his dinner guests, he did not want to refuse her. So he immediately sent an executioner with orders to bring John's head. The man went, beheaded John in the prison, and brought back his head on a platter. He presented it to the girl, and she gave it to her mother. On hearing of this, John's disciples came and took his body and laid it in a tomb.

Consider This

So what's all the fuss about Herod's marriage? Warning: this is definitely TV-MA.

Herod the Great had a son, Aristobulus, who later went on to have a daughter. Her name was Herodias.

Herod the Great had another son, known as Herod II, who later married Herodias. Yes, that means she married her uncle. Together they had a daughter named Salome, the "stripper" making an appearance in today's text.

Herod the Great had yet another son, known as Antipas, who was the Herod at issue in today's text. This Herodian dynasty had more of a family forest than a family tree.

As the story goes, Antipas visited Rome to see his brother Herod II at which time he apparently stole his wife, Herodias.

Did I mention Antipas was already married? No problem—nothing a quick divorce can't solve, right?

Now, if I've got my facts right, Antipas was not only stealing his brother's wife, he was also marrying his niece. It seems by any standards to call this an "illicit" marriage would be more than warranted. For Jews, it would have been outright anathema. Why? I was with a friend yesterday who put it this way: "Marriage is not about marriage. Marriage is about God."

So you've got the picture. Herodias and Salome set up shop in the palace of Antipas. When John got wind of this, he went ballistic. Why did John have to rail against this illicit and adulterous marriage? Because marriage is not about marriage. Marriage is about God. It would have been a lot easier for John to have gone about his seemingly more important business of heralding God's kingdom than taking issue with a politician's marriage. At minimum, he would have "kept a good head on his shoulders" a lot longer. John, however, held an uncompromising conviction about marriage being about God, making an offense against marriage an offense against God. He could not be silent.

Because of Antipas's appreciation for John, we might reasonably assume John was making headway with him on this front. Why else would Herodias and Salome hate John so much. They were the ones who stood to lose everything. Who knows, Antipas may have eventually repented. They weren't taking any chances. They wanted his head.

So Herodias and Salome (a.k.a. Antipas's wife and step-daughter, a.k.a. Antipas's niece and grandniece) hatched a plan. Herodias sent Salome to do a sexy dance for her grand-uncle. Apparently, Uncle Antipas had quite the fetish for dirty dancing, and surely he'd had way too much to drink. He pledged to his stepdaughter/grandniece anything she wanted up to half of his kingdom. My immediate response to such an offer: "I'll take half of your kingdom." To show you how powerful was the toxic mix of fear and hatred, they chose revenge. Instead of a massive trust fund for Salome, Herodias opted for John's head.

Okay, there's a small problem I failed to note. Antipas's former wife, the one he divorced, was an Arabian princess. That means her father was an Arabian king. It's never a good thing to have an Arabian king mad at you, especially because you dumped his daughter. This king declared war on Antipas and it cost him dearly.

So what's the point of pointing all this out? Marriage matters. Marriage is not about marriage. Marriage is about God. For those of us who are married, we need to make our own marriage matter by making our marriage about God. A final word of caution: Don't be afraid to share them, but be careful with your convictions about marriage. They could cost you your head.

The Prayer

Spirit of the living God, fall afresh on me.

The Questions

- If marriage is not about marriage but about God, what implications does this have for you? For marriage? For the church? For the culture?

32 The Holy Spirit and Setting Boundaries

MARK 6:30–37 ESV | The apostles returned to Jesus and told him all that they had done and taught. And he said to them, "Come away by yourselves to a desolate place and rest a while." For many were coming and going, and they had no leisure even to eat. And they went away in the boat to a desolate place by themselves. Now many saw them going and recognized them, and they ran there on foot from all the towns and got there ahead of them. When he went ashore he saw a great crowd, and he had compassion on them, because they were like sheep without a shepherd. And he began to teach them many things. And when it grew late, his disciples came to him and said, "This is a desolate place, and the hour is now late. Send them away to go into the surrounding countryside and villages and buy themselves something to eat." But he answered them, "You give them something to eat." And they said to him, "Shall we go and buy two hundred denarii worth of bread and give it to them to eat?"

Consider This

Today's text opens with a remark about the insane schedule of Jesus and his disciples. There was so much going on they did not even have a chance to eat. Their lives were likely getting thin and moving toward the ragged edge. How do I know this? Because of the way Jesus responded to them. He said, *"Come away by yourselves to a desolate place and rest a while."*

That sounds good, doesn't it—getting away with a small group of friends to a quiet place to hang out with Jesus? When is the last time that happened for you? I'm trying to remember. The press of life never stops and it never will stop. Even when you enter into so-called retirement it never stops—which can be a good thing, right?

What happened in today's text is a real marker of the ministry of the Holy Spirit. When the Spirit is abiding among a people in a palpable way, you can't keep others away. The gravity of the Spirit pulls them in like a tractor beam. The Holy Spirit never tires of this, but human beings do. Even Jesus got tired. If he didn't, we would know he was not fully human.

Note how when the disciples got in the boats to head for the hills, the people ran after them along the shore. This demonstrates the profound human hunger to be encountered by the Holy Spirit. Most interesting to me about today's text is the way Jesus responds to the people. Here's their chance to take a much-deserved break with Jesus and they arrive at their retreat only to find hordes of people (thousands, even) waiting for them. The technical term for such an occurrence is "bummer."

When he went ashore he saw a great crowd, and he had compassion on them, because they were like sheep without a shepherd. And he began to teach them many things.

Compassion is an expression of the Holy Spirit. Charity often comes from feeling sorry for people. Compassion only comes from feeling sorry with people. Another interesting observation is the way the Holy Spirit expresses compassion in this situation—through the ministry of teaching them "many things." Note the way teaching is connected to shepherding. All of this should be a deep encouragement to teachers of every sort, especially school teachers. Doesn't this capture the calling of a teacher—to compassionately shepherd people by teaching them many things?

Now to the point. The time came for supper and instead of enjoying a nice meal around the campfire with Jesus, the disciples are having to concern themselves with feeding five thousand people. This is nuts! Jesus adds the last straw when he tells his disciples to give them something to eat. Absurd! He pushes them so far past their human limits that their heads were spinning. He's stretching their capacity beyond their own good intentions so they will learn to minister in the compassion of the Holy Spirit. He's about to set up an extraordinary teaching moment for his disciples.

Unless our capacity gets stretched, we can stay stuck in our own abilities for a long time. This is where boundaries come into play. Jesus was taking these guys for a much-needed break and now he has them scrambling around to figure out how to feed five thousand people! In present-day terms, Jesus made an intentional move to set a healthy boundary for himself and his followers and the people ran right over it. They always do. There is no end to human need and there is no end to the capacity of the Holy Spirit, but there is a definite end to our human ability. The trouble is that we don't usually know that end until it's too late and we're burned out. The problem when burned-out, over-tired people try to set boundaries occurs when they wind up crafting desperate strategies to protect themselves from other people instead. We call them "walls" and they keep other people out by isolating ourselves in.

There's a better way. Boundaries are not about protecting ourselves from people. Healthy boundaries prepare us *for* people. Jesus had little boundaries all over the place. Early in the morning he would go to that solitary place to pray and its distinctive effect caused his disciples to ask him to teach them to pray. He put a ban on fasting while he was with his disciples so they would know fasting was about fellowship with him when they were physically apart. He reinstalled the factory settings on Sabbath-keeping as a boundary for the sake of people rather than a legalistic religious observance for God. He taught them to eat and drink in remembrance of him and in these smallest portions would come the greatest nourishment. And, yes, he did his best to take them on staff retreats to debrief and unwind even though people still needed help.

Healthy boundaries set us free from the trap of thinking we are responsible for people and free us up to be responsible to people. Healthy boundaries are not about saying no to people so you can say yes to yourself. They are more about saying yes to yourself in the name of Jesus so you can say yes to people in the power of the Holy Spirit. I think for Jesus, setting boundaries is a way of being obedient to the limitless Holy Spirit so the Holy Spirit can work amazing grace through our limitations instead of despite them.

The Prayer

Spirit of the living God, fall afresh on me.

The Questions

- What does our failure to set good boundaries say about our view of ourselves? What does it say about our actual faith in Jesus?

33 Awakening to the Miracle That Never Stops

MARK 6:37–44 NRSV | But he answered them, "You give them something to eat." They said to him, "Are we to go and buy two hundred denarii worth of bread, and give it to them to eat?" And he said to them, "How many loaves have you? Go and see." When they had found out, they said, "Five, and two fish." Then he ordered them to get all the people to sit down in groups on the green grass. So they sat down in groups of hundreds and of fifties. Taking the five loaves and the two fish, he looked up to heaven, and blessed and broke the loaves, and gave them to his disciples to set before the people; and he divided the two fish among them all. And all ate and were filled; and they took up twelve baskets full of broken pieces and of the fish. Those who had eaten the loaves numbered five thousand men.

Consider This

When faced with a big challenge or problem, our first impulse usually involves some kind of calculation of how much money it would take to solve the problem. I think this is part of why Jesus pitched the problem to the disciples, to see how they would solve it. Predictably, they got out their calculators and determined it would cost half a year's wages. Somehow I think Jesus was hoping they might remember that great catch of fish he engineered; the one that almost sank two boats. I think Jesus probably hoped they might appeal to him for help. There's a good word in here for us when faced with large challenges—start with Jesus. Entreating the Lord is not a last-ditch effort, it's the starting point.

There's an even better approach. Take on challenges so large that if Jesus doesn't intervene you will fail. The disciples saw a problem. Jesus saw people. Yesterday's text captured the heart of God for the human race: "He had compassion on them, because they were like sheep without a shepherd" (v. 34).

If I had been one of those disciples, I would have been looking at my watch, wondering when this thing would finally end so we could get on with our plans. Remember, this was unplanned. Compassion is not a pre-planned mission trip (though these can be filled with compassion). Compassion is a Holy Spirit formed disposition deep within one's inner person. As Jesus constantly demonstrates, compassion is the nature of God. Compassion is not what we do with our loose change. It's a way of being deeply attuned to other people, seeing past their need and into their nature. Compassion happens when the brokenness of the image of God in me beholds the brokenness of the image of God in another. It moves me from the posture of "helping a brother out," to the place of holding a brother's pain. It's hard. It costs us a lot more than money. It requires giving ourselves away.

Compassion is to charity as a long steady rain is to a water sprinkler. This is precisely what God is like. This is who the Holy Spirit is making us to be. It's not about giving more, as good as that may be. Compassion is about becoming a new kind of person. Even as I write, I find myself asking, *Do I really want to become compassionate?* Half a year's wages actually sounds a lot easier. It makes me realize how giving money can be such a substitutionary charade for true generosity.

Finally, we come to the miracle. I'm beginning to think this is exactly what Jesus had in mind from the get-go. The retreat was a holy ruse. Why do I think that? The text was careful to tell us earlier about the extreme demands and out-of-control activity of the disciples. They had been pushed past their limits. Then he invites them on a retreat only to follow it with a request to feed five thousand people. The conditions were perfect for something of a miraculous object lesson.

First, Jesus gave the Twelve a picture of what real limitations and scarce resources look like: five loaves and two fish. (Imagine trying to feed fifty kids with a single hotdog.) I think the bigger comparison here is between these meager rations and twelve helpers.

Second, he has them sit down in groups of hundreds and fifties. Why do we need to know this detail? I think it's because he wanted the disciples to know this detail. How else would we know there were five thousand people there? This is not a preacher's inflated estimate of the attendance on Easter Sunday.

Third, Jesus doesn't balk at the impossibility of the challenge at hand.

Taking the five loaves and the two fish, he looked up to heaven, and blessed and broke the loaves, and gave them to his disciples to set before the people; and he divided the two fish among them all.

He did exactly what he does at every meal. Four moves: He took. He blessed. He broke. He gave. There's a hidden curiosity here though. The verbs "took," "blessed," and "broke" are past tense verbs. "Gave" translates into English as past tense but the Greek text renders this in the imperfect tense. The imperfect verb tense points to an action done in the past that keeps on moving indefinitely into the future. In other words, the fishes and loaves were being continuously multiplied in his hands. It's not like all of a sudden five thousand fish and ten thousand loaves materialized on the scene. No, the miracle was happening over and over and over and over again in the movement from his hands to theirs.

The crowd didn't see this, but the disciples couldn't have missed it. I think this is the point. Just like those meager rations, so were these disciples, but upon being offered to Jesus something extraordinary happened. He would bless them and break them and make them a gift to the world—an unending source of extravagant, compassionate generosity.

These four verbs would present themselves again at the most mysterious, miraculous, meaningful meal in the history of the world.

> While they were eating, Jesus took bread, and when he had given thanks, he broke it and gave it to his disciples, saying, "Take it; this is my body."
>
> Then he took a cup, and when he had given thanks, he gave it to them, and they all drank from it.
>
> "This is my blood of the covenant, which is poured out for many," he said to them. (Mark 14:22–24)

Are you seeing it? As he is the bread, in his hands we are the bread—blessed, broken, and given, and given, and given, and given. Discipleship is all about learning to live our lives in his hands. And the miracle after the miracle is there is always more than enough left for us.

The Prayer

Spirit of the living God, fall afresh on me.

The Questions

- What keeps you from releasing control of yourself and surrendering completely to Jesus? What would be the sign to Jesus and to yourself that you have surrendered?

The Disciples' Dilemma: When Knowledge Gets in the Way of Knowing

34

MARK 6:45–52 | Immediately Jesus made his disciples get into the boat and go on ahead of him to Bethsaida, while he dismissed the crowd. After leaving them, he went up on a mountainside to pray.

Later that night, the boat was in the middle of the lake, and he was alone on land. He saw the disciples straining at the oars, because the wind was against them. Shortly before dawn he went out to them, walking on the lake. He was about to pass by them, but when they saw him walking on the lake, they thought he was a ghost. They cried out, because they all saw him and were terrified.

Immediately he spoke to them and said, "Take courage! It is I. Don't be afraid." Then he climbed into the boat with them, and

the wind died down. They were completely amazed, for they had
not understood about the loaves; their hearts were hardened.

Consider This

I want us to notice something about Jesus' daily ways of
being and doing life. He stays in constant contact with his
Father. No sooner had the disciples picked up the leftover
bread, when Jesus hurries them into the boat and back across
the lake. Only he did not go with them. Why did Jesus not go
with the disciples?

After leaving them, he went up on a mountainside to pray.

Like me, you may be wondering why Jesus didn't take his
disciples with him on his mountainside prayer retreat. I have
a theory on this. Let me preface it by pointing out the specu-
lative nature of it. As I noted yesterday, I don't think Jesus
ever intended to take the disciples to a quiet place to get some
rest. That was a ruse. Jesus knew the mob would follow them.
He had the miracle of the fish and loaves already planned.
Come on. This is Jesus we are talking about. Jesus was setting
the disciples up for an inescapable experience of his divine
nature. We must remember, while it comes easier for us
to think of Jesus in the category of the divine, those early
disciples saw a bona fide human being when they looked at
Jesus. Put yourself in their shoes. How on earth could they
have understood him as the God of the universe? To perform
acts of healing and deliverance were one thing. But it didn't
follow that he was God. To feed five thousand people with
five loaves and two fish could be considered a marvel, but

it wouldn't necessarily mean he was God. Think about it. It would take a lot to convince you that a person you knew was the God of the cosmos.

Mark's gospel is a bit of a "Who is this guy?" mystery. The demons knew immediately and he silenced them. He didn't want the disciples to learn of his identity from Satan. In the end, we will see a Roman centurion get the revelation. Through it all Jesus was somewhat systematically leaving a trail of revelatory bread crumbs for his disciples so they might awaken to the reality of his divinity. He wanted them to get it.

The same is true today. He wants us to get it, not by acquiring knowledge but through the Holy Spirit revealing him to us. The trouble is that we have a hard time learning what we think we already know. As I reflect on my own experience, it strikes me that I had a lot of knowledge about Jesus long before I actually knew him. And the more knowledge I accumulated about Jesus the harder it became to admit that I did not know him.

Here's an example. I could become the most-renown expert in the world on avocados without ever eating a single avocado. I could tell you everything about an avocado except what it was like to taste one. But the minute I taste an avocado all of a sudden something I could never have known is revealed to me in the experience. In fact, the experience of eating an avocado would likely illuminate so much of what I had already learned about them that I could share with you even more about avocados than I thought I knew before. At the point of tasting, my commitment to being an authority on avocados would transform into a surprising love and devotion to them. I would move from an avocado authority to an avocado evangelist. I'll pause the analogy there because I think you see the point.

Many things can be learned about and from another human being, but a human being is actually God—this can only be revealed. This is why Jesus taught in parables. Parables created a context where truth could be revealed and experienced rather than merely learned and controlled. The truth is, from way back then to the present day, nothing has changed except that we have the benefit of hindsight. Still, our hindsight is at best only knowledge about Jesus. The crux of the matter comes down to this question: Have we experienced the reality of the grace and love of God in Jesus Christ by the revelation of the Holy Spirit? I'm not asking if you know the date and time when you received salvation. I'm asking if you have actually tasted the love of God in Jesus Christ through the person of the Holy Spirit? "Taste and see that the LORD is good; blessed is the one who takes refuge in him" (Ps. 34:8).

There are many people who have rejected Jesus because they have never actually tasted his goodness. In fact, they have a bad taste in their mouth from their experience of people who may have known a lot about Jesus, but probably didn't actually know him themselves. This, in part, is the dangerous phenomenon of Pharisaism. We were not made to learn a lot of stuff about God, as helpful as that can be, but to know God intimately in our everyday experience. That's why Jesus goes to the mountainside to pray, to enjoy uninterrupted fellowship with his Father.

Paul captures this idea in his prayer for us. Read this text carefully.

> I pray that out of his glorious riches he may strengthen you with power through his Spirit in your inner being, so that Christ may dwell in your hearts through faith. And I pray that you, being rooted and established in love, may have power, together with all the Lord's holy people, to grasp how wide and long and high and deep is the love of Christ, and to know this love that surpasses knowledge—that you may be filled to the measure of all the fullness of God. (Eph. 3:16–19)

The great danger for the disciples of Jesus, then and now, is to become too prideful to admit that our knowing (experience) has not caught up with our knowledge. It produces the problem Jesus was trying to break through: *for they had not understood about the loaves; their hearts were hardened.*

Getting back to the matter at hand, I think this sending of the disciples to cross the lake was another setup. He knew they hadn't gotten it back at the big meal; that they had probably filed the event as a superhuman marvel. He knew it would take them all night to get across the lake, which would give him plenty of time to process this situation with his Father on the mountainside. Something tells me Jesus knew he needed to speak to his Father a lot more about his disciples before he spoke a lot more to his disciples about his Father.

Throughout the Bible, from the opening waters of chaos in Genesis 1, to the parting of the sea for Israel, to the raging waters referenced throughout the Psalms, to his most recent calming of the storm—a hallmark of divine sovereignty is the demonstration of control over nature (particularly the seas). Jesus walking across the waters was yet another attempt to reveal his divinity to his disciples, to create an inescapable revelatory experience of his God-ness (and goodness).

All of this has me asking about the state of my own heart. Is it revelation-proof? Or might I find the humility to make an offering to Jesus of all I have learned about him, asking him for the grace to transform my knowledge into knowing?

The Prayer

Spirit of the living God, fall afresh on me.

The Questions

- Are you in need of a deeper humility before God and others when it comes to the things of God?
- Do you see how it is hard to learn what you think you already know?

Do We Really Recognize Jesus?

35

MARK 6:53–56 ESV | When they had crossed over, they came to land at Gennesaret and moored to the shore. And when they got out of the boat, the people immediately recognized him and ran about the whole region and began to bring the sick people on their beds to wherever they heard he was. And wherever he came, in villages, cities, or countryside, they laid the sick in the marketplaces and implored him that they might touch even the fringe of his garment. And as many as touched it were made well.

Consider This

Let's begin by relocating ourselves in the text with a kind of biblical GPS approach. It's something we need to do often. Life moves so steadily past us that we often find ourselves going from one thing to the next and losing touch with what life is about in the first place. I'm convinced this is part of the reason God commanded us to keep Sabbath, but that's for another discussion.

In the warp and woof of daily Scripture reading, it's all too easy to keep up with what page we're on, yet lose touch with what story we're in. What if I sent you a Google map that showed you my location within about a one-mile radius; would you know where I was? Well, yes and no. We can only know where we are in a meaningful sense by knowing the larger geographical context in which we are situated. You would need to zoom out a few clicks to see the town, county, state, and so forth. As an interesting aside, we can only know who we are by knowing the larger relational context in which we are associated.

We can only meaningfully understand what is going on in the Bible by understanding and staying in touch with the larger biblical story in which we are situated. We are in Mark's gospel, which began by locating us in the wilderness with John the Baptist where we quickly met John who baptized Jesus. At this baptism, we had the privilege of witnessing the Holy Spirit descend from heaven with the voice of the Father saying, "You are my Son, whom I love; with you I am well pleased" (Mark 1:11). In the next scene the demons are calling him "the Holy One of God" (Mark 1:24). Beyond that, no one gets who he is. Some call him teacher. Others know him as a healer. His family thinks he's out of his mind. The Pharisees actually call him Satan. In the previous text, he served as something of a first-century food truck. And his disciples—the closest ultimate insiders—they aren't getting it either. And his hometown people can't see past him being the son of his parents.

Mark's gospel has us on a journey of discovery. Who recognizes who Jesus really is and who does not? So we come to today's text where we get this:

And when they got out of the boat, the people immediately recognized him.

No, they didn't. They recognized the man who had miraculous powers to heal, who could raise the dead, who commanded the demons, who had authority unlike the teachers of the law, but they did not recognize him as the Son of God. Had they recognized him as the God of the universe, they would have hit the deck, bowing as low as they possibly could in an act of humble adoration. You know what they did instead? The text is clear: they ran.

They recognized him for what he could do, not for who he was, and they ran. Sure, it was awesome that they ran throughout the countryside finding people in need and carrying them to Jesus to heal. That's a measure of faith to be sure. But what would it look like for faith to be placed in who he is, beyond just in what he could do?

I think that's what he was looking for. I think that's still what he is looking for. Jesus is looking for people who recognize not only his goodness, but his God-ness.

The interesting thing about when we begin recognizing Jesus for who he is and not just for what he can do, we will discover he recognizes us not on what we can or can't do, but on who we are. Even better, we will find ourselves recognizing people for who they are and not for what they can or can't do.

The Prayer

Spirit of the living God, fall afresh on me.

The Questions

- How would you describe who Jesus is to you beyond his mercies and gifts and blessings upon you?

36 When the Holy Spirit Does Something Not in the Bulletin

MARK 7:1–8 NRSV | Now when the Pharisees and some of the scribes who had come from Jerusalem gathered around him, they noticed that some of his disciples were eating with defiled hands, that is, without washing them. (For the Pharisees, and all the Jews, do not eat unless they thoroughly wash their hands, thus observing the tradition of the elders; and they do not eat anything from the market unless they wash it; and there are also many other traditions that they observe, the washing of cups, pots, and bronze kettles.) So the Pharisees and the scribes asked him, "Why do your disciples not live according to the tradition of the elders, but eat with defiled hands?" He said to them, "Isaiah prophesied rightly about you hypocrites, as it is written, 'This people honors me with their lips, but their hearts are far from me; in vain do they worship me, teaching human precepts as doctrines.'

You abandon the commandment of God and hold to human tradition."

Consider This

It's important to get the scene from the previous entry clearly in our minds.

"And wherever he went—into villages, towns or countryside—they placed the sick in the marketplaces. They begged him to let them touch even the edge of his cloak, and all who touched it were healed" (Mark 6:56).

An absolute Holy Spirit phenomenon swept across the land. People ran all over the countryside bringing their sick and demon-possessed family and friends to Jesus. Blind eyes finally glimpsed the beauty of their own children. Lame people danced in jubilation. Deaf ears heard the sound of music for the first time. Poor people could hardly comprehend the extravagant scope of the good news.

News had reached Jerusalem of the amazing grace spreading across the land. Headquarters (a.k.a. the temple) dispatched a delegation of officials to see the unfolding miraculous events with their own eyes. Surely they would embrace Jesus and invite him into their fellowship.

Now, with this scene of extraordinary proportions in your mind's eye, behold what happened next: *Pharisees and some of the scribes who had come from Jerusalem gathered around him, they noticed that some of his disciples were eating with defiled hands, that is, without washing them. . . . So the Pharisees and the scribes asked him, "Why do your disciples not live according to the tradition of the elders, but eat with defiled hands?"*

You've got to be kidding me. Dead people are being raised to life again and the religious leadership can only seem to notice Jesus' disciples aren't washing their hands before dinner.

It's how human nature works. Here's what I mean by that. People typically want to control what they don't understand—especially people who have power or authority and especially people who are considered authorities—whether they actually have real authority or not.

Whenever the Holy Spirit does what the Holy Spirit does best—which is to reverse the curse of sin and death—the masses tend to embrace it. Unfortunately, the classes tend to get up in arms about it. I've been at the First Methodist Church when the Holy Spirit started coloring outside of the lines. Deliverance and healing broke out at the altar. People experienced freedom from bondages that had held them for decades. Yes, there were some out-of-the-ordinary expressions never before witnessed by most people present, yet they mostly remained open. The most-surprising reactions came from the religious authorities. In fact, they did everything in their power to shut it down. The leaders of the meeting were branded heretics (though no one ever identified the particular heresy).

When I read a text like today's, all of a sudden it's not so surprising what happened back then. When the Holy Spirit goes to work, it can get messy. It can be less than dignified in the eyes of sophisticated church people, but it can be a downright threat to the leadership.

So when's the last time you remember the Holy Spirit doing something that was not in the bulletin? Could it be possible our own posture of openness or closed-ness has something to do with this? We need not be afraid of the person and work of the Holy Spirit. Sure, we need wise leaders who can tell the difference between the Holy Spirit's movement and out-of-control wildfire and who can shepherd us with grace and truth. More than anything, though, we need to develop the humility to let God be God.

So here's the question I'm asking myself: Am I completely open to the work of the Holy Spirit in my life? Even if I don't understand it? Even if it makes me uncomfortable? Even if it means I am out of control?

The Prayer

Spirit of the living God, fall afresh on me.

The Questions

- Do you tend to be a person who leans in to what might be the movement of the Spirit of God—with self-abandonment? Or do you tend to be one who leans away—with self-protection?
- How can we learn to discern without needing to be so in control?

37 The Problem with the Rules . . . or the Possibilities

MARK 7:9–15 | And he continued, "You have a fine way of setting aside the commands of God in order to observe your own traditions! For Moses said, 'Honor your father and mother,' and, 'Anyone who curses their father or mother is to be put to death.' But you say that if anyone declares that what might have been used to help their father or mother is Corban (that is, devoted to God)—then you no longer let them do anything for their father or mother. Thus you nullify the word of God by your tradition that you have handed down. And you do many things like that."

Again Jesus called the crowd to him and said, "Listen to me, everyone, and understand this. Nothing outside a person can defile them by going into them. Rather, it is what comes out of a person that defiles them."

Consider This

I would like to go back to the previous text and a passage, which sheds light on this text as well as the larger principle at work.

In response to the hand-washing complaint, Jesus offered this.

He replied, "Isaiah was right when he prophesied about you hypocrites; as it is written:

'These people honor me with their lips,
  but their hearts are far from me.
They worship me in vain;
    their teachings are merely human rules.'"
(Mark 7:6–7)

Sometimes you can get the "A" and still fail the course.

There's the letter of the Law and then there's the spirit of the Law. The Law will lead in one of two directions and it depends on who is handling the Law. The Law will move according to the dictates of the letter or in keeping with the spirit behind it. The Pharisees are clearly moving in the legalistic direction. They are trying to catch Jesus in some kind of breach of the Law. They are gotcha people, and people who are gotcha people also believe in a gotcha God.

Take it out of a religious context and put it into a work context. Have you ever had a gotcha boss? When employees have this type of boss, they stick exceedingly close to the policy manual. They play the CYA game. Maybe you have a gotcha spouse. In the game of gotcha, it's all about the rules and keeping the letter of the law and covering your rear and being ready to justify your actions. It's a horrible way to live. No one thinks about the mission anymore; only appeasing the boss or the spouse or the god. This is how legalism works. The Law is wielded as a sword.

What appears to make them important and use their laws or ministered wishes.

The outcome of legalism is "honoring me with their lips but their hearts are far from me." So what would it mean to honor God and the Law of God with our hearts? It would mean seeing a different kind of God—not a gotcha God but a for-you God. God is not out to get us. God is out to help us. God is for us, not against us. Behind every precept of God is the spirit of love. Far from a sword in God's hands against us, the Law becomes his shield of protection for us.

Again Jesus called the crowd to him and said, "Listen to me, everyone, and understand this. Nothing outside a person can defile them by going into them. Rather, it is what comes out of a person that defiles them."

The way to life is not external conformity to the letter, but deep internal transformation by the Spirit.

Are you a gotcha person? Is it all about conformity to the policy manual? Or are you a for-others person? It's not a matter of Law or no Law. It's a matter of Law as a sword or a shield? What you believe about God will determine the direction you go with this.

He has made us competent as ministers of a new covenant—not of the letter but of the Spirit; for the letter kills, but the Spirit gives life. (2 Cor. 3:6)

The Prayer
Spirit of the living God, fall afresh on me.

The Questions

• What is it deep inside that makes us want to cover ourselves and prove other people wrong?

[handwritten: An insincere heart filled with ourselves — important — Wanting to always to be right]

Getting to the Heart of the Matter

38

MARK 7:17–23 ESV | And when he had entered the house and left the people, his disciples asked him about the parable. And he said to them, "Then are you also without understanding? Do you not see that whatever goes into a person from outside cannot defile him, since it enters not his heart but his stomach, and is expelled?" (Thus he declared all foods clean.) And he said, "What comes out of a person is what defiles him. For from within, out of the heart of man, come evil thoughts, sexual immorality, theft, murder, adultery, coveting, wickedness, deceit, sensuality, envy, slander, pride, foolishness. All these evil things come from within, and they defile a person."

Consider This

Scripture uses the term "heart" some eight hundred times yet never to refer to the physical organ that pumps blood through the body. The point is to demonstrate the essential, volitional, willful core of a human person. It's what matters most. This is what is broken about our human condition.

This is the focus of the Holy Spirit in the work of restoring us to the image of God. Recall Paul's prayer in his letter to the Ephesians:

> I pray that the eyes of your heart may be enlightened in order that you may know the hope to which he has called you, the riches of his glorious inheritance in his holy people, and his incomparably great power for us who believe. (Eph. 1:18–19)

Jesus brings laser-like focus to the heart. Remember in the Sermon on the Mount (a.k.a. the Kingdom Manifesto) when he said, "Blessed are the pure in heart, for they will see God" (Matt. 5:8)? He spoke of murder as beginning with nursing anger in one's heart and adultery as harboring lust in one's heart.

In today's text, he cuts to the heart of the matter of human brokenness when he says: *"For from within, out of the heart of man, come evil thoughts."* It's why the Proverbs speak so often of the heart with words like, "Above all else, guard your heart, for everything you do flows from it" (Prov. 4:23).

Back in the days of John and Charles Wesley, the classic question of those in fellowship with each other was, How is it with your soul? Today we might more commonly hear, How's your heart?

Remember the words of the psalmist, who put it so succinctly, "Who may ascend the mountain of the Lord? Who may stand in his holy place? The one who has clean hands and a pure heart, who does not trust in an idol or swear by a false god" (Ps. 24:3–4).

By the pen of Jeremiah, the Holy Spirit issues this stern warning,

> The heart is deceitful above all things
>> and beyond cure.
>> Who can understand it?
> "I the LORD search the heart
>> and examine the mind,
> to reward each person according to their conduct,
>> according to what their deeds deserve." (17:9–10)

I'll close with one of the great prayers from the *Book of Common Prayer*. It's called the "Collect for Purity." I'd encourage you to commit this one to memory and pray it regularly.

> Almighty God, to you all hearts are open, all desires known and from you no secrets are hid. Cleanse the thoughts of our hearts by the inspiration of your Holy Spirit that we may perfectly love you and worthily magnify your holy name, through Jesus Christ our Lord, Amen.[4]

Note the prayer's honesty with respect to sin. Even more so, look at the sheer audacity of the request—to perfectly love God. Wow!

---

4. "The Collect for Purity," Episcopal Church, *The Book of Common Prayer and Administration of the Sacraments and Other Rights and Ceremonies of the Church: Together with the Psalter of Psalms of David According to the Use of the Episcopal Church* (New York: Seabury Press, 1979).

Cleanse the thoughts of our hearts, Lord. Yes, cleanse the thoughts of our hearts.

The Prayer

Spirit of the living God, fall afresh on me.

The Questions

- How is your heart? Pure? Cloudy? Anxious? Joyful? Troubled? Peaceful?
- How can you stay in touch with the state of your heart?

39 The Desperate Need We Have to Be in Need

MARK 7:24–30 NRSV | From there he set out and went away to the region of Tyre. He entered a house and did not want anyone to know he was there. Yet he could not escape notice, but a woman whose little daughter had an unclean spirit immediately heard about him, and she came and bowed down at his feet. Now the woman was a Gentile, of Syrophoenician origin. She begged him to cast the demon out of her daughter. He said to her, "Let the children be fed first, for it is not fair to take the children's food and throw it to the dogs." But she answered him, "Sir, even the dogs under the table eat the children's crumbs." Then he said to her, "For saying that, you may go—the demon has left your daughter."

Jesus - 1st priority was to feed the children
Teaching his Disciple - Not to let pets
interrupt the meal. She was a gentle

So she went home, found the child lying on the bed, and the demon gone.

Consider This

Jesus, still in search of respite for himself and his disciples, left Galilee and crossed over into Gentile territory. He tried desperately to keep his presence there quiet but to no avail. A Gentile woman apparently knew Jesus' reputation. She was desperate to get help for her daughter who was possessed by a demon.

This interaction between Jesus and the woman sounds somewhat harsh to modern readers; however, there's something of a cultural inside idiom at play here. The word that comes to mind to describe Jesus' tone and demeanor is "cheeky." When the woman responded as she did, Jesus responded back with a kind of "touché."

The big deal in today's text is the faith of the woman. First, she fell at his feet. Second, she pleaded with Jesus to heal her daughter. Third, Jesus prayed no prayer, spoke no particular words of deliverance or exorcism. He didn't ask to see the daughter. He merely told the woman the demon had left her daughter and to go. And she went. She simply believed Jesus and acted in response.

This is the kind of faith Jesus is looking for. We've seen it before in Mark. The interesting thing is where he is finding this faith. The religious leaders opposed him. His disciples weren't grasping who he was. Bottom line: the ones we would expect to get it didn't and the one's we would least expect to get it did.

One final thought: the people who most get Jesus are the ones who find themselves most in touch with their need of him. Jesus' Kingdom Manifesto comes to mind again, particularly the opening line, "Blessed are the poor in spirit, for theirs is the kingdom of heaven" (Matt. 5:3).

Poverty of spirit comes from knowing one's need of God. The most interesting thing to me is the thing I've never noticed before. Of all the people in Jesus' orbit, it's his own disciples who don't seem to be that in need of him; to embody poverty of spirit. One can claim to be a disciple of Jesus without really knowing their need of him. It causes me to examine myself along these lines. And you?

The Prayer

Spirit of the living God, fall afresh on me.

The Questions

- How aware are you of your need of God?
- Does your awareness tend to rise and fall with the level of your problems and challenges or has it gotten deeper than that?

Sermon on the mount - The Kingdom of Heaven has come. God is with us. He cares for us. He heals not only physical but spiritual. No sin to great & small to him. Jesus Words offer freedom, hope, peace of heart & eternal life with God.

128.

The Difference between Extravagant Embrace and Radical Inclusiveness

40

MARK 7:31–37 | Then Jesus left the vicinity of Tyre and went through Sidon, down to the Sea of Galilee and into the region of the Decapolis. There some people brought to him a man who was deaf and could hardly talk, and they begged Jesus to place his hand on him.

After he took him aside, away from the crowd, Jesus put his fingers into the man's ears. Then he spit and touched the man's tongue. He looked up to heaven and with a deep sigh said to him, "Ephphatha!" (which means "Be opened!"). At this, the man's ears were opened, his tongue was loosened and he began to speak plainly.

Jesus commanded them not to tell anyone. But the more he did so, the more they kept talking about it. People were overwhelmed with amazement. "He has done everything well," they said. "He even makes the deaf hear and the mute speak."

Consider This

For those who haven't paid much attention to biblical geography, which is most people, let's begin today by getting our geographical bearings. Galilee is in the northern part of the country. Jerusalem was in the south. Jesus spent most of his time in and around Galilee. Yesterday, we went with Jesus and his disciples on their quest for rest to Tyre. Tyre was north of Galilee and in the southern portion of what today is Lebanon.

In today's text, Jesus left Tyre and headed for the Sea of Galilee. When he reached the sea, he took a left and went into the Decapolis. Had he taken a right he would have landed back in Galilee. The Decapolis consisted of ten cities located primarily on the eastern side of the Jordan River located in what today is the nation of Jordan. While Tyre was Phoenician in its culture, the Decapolis was decisively Greco-Roman. In the midst of a largely Semitic region, the Decapolis was a stronghold for Greek and Roman culture.

Why does this matter? The demands on Jesus and his disciples were extraordinary. At the same time, opposition from the religious establishment was on the rise. Jesus literally "left the building," so to speak. He headed for the border, out of the land of the Jews and into Gentile country, where it turned out he was also fairly well-known. Before we get halfway through the Gospel According to Mark, the gospel has already gone out of bounds. (Okay, it went out of bounds a long time ago with the sorts of people Jesus healed and fellowshipped with within the promised land.)

All the boundaries that matter so much to people, then and now, Jesus seemed to ignore. Jesus moved without hesitation across boundaries of status, race, gender, ritual laws, unclean-ness, Sabbath prohibitions, and more. Next, he ignored national borders and cultural boundaries. It's like they weren't there.

Two things are always simultaneously true of Jesus, then and now. He never hesitates to call sin "sin," and he never hesitates to embrace people. The only two things Jesus cannot abide is calling sin "not sin," and failing to embrace people. Whether it be the fierce legalism of the religious elite or the audacious license of the cultural zeitgeist, Jesus will always call sin "sin." It's like calling cancer "cancer." In the same way, a human body cannot tolerate cancer, a human being cannot tolerate sin. Both mean death. When sin is called "not sin," it is akin to looking at a malignant tumor and calling it "benign."

Somewhere along the way the extravagant embrace of the gospel in the name of Jesus became twisted into the radical doctrines of political correctness in the name of inclusiveness. In this ideological framework, the only sin is to be intolerant of sin. It breeds a culture of death. This is how tolerance in the name of love actually kills love.

The embrace of the gospel always leads, sooner or later, to the exclusion of sin and ultimately to the end of death. It's because the gospel is about salvation, which means healing, which means the eradication of the cancer that is sin and death. This is how love wins.

So why all of this conversation about sin coming out of a text that doesn't even mention sin? Because this text, among other things, is about boundaries and this is where all the confusion and chaos creeps in. Jesus does not eradicate boundaries in the interest of inclusiveness. He crosses boundaries in the name of love.

The Prayer

Spirit of the living God, fall afresh on me.

The Questions

- Do you see how the tolerance of sin is the antithesis of love and the pinnacle of deception? What is the strategy of love to combat this deception?
- How might we be deceived in our approach to combatting this radical tolerance and inclusiveness of our time?

41 On the Everyday Ministry of Eating

MARK 8:1–10 ESV | In those days, when again a great crowd had gathered, and they had nothing to eat, he called his disciples to him and said to them, "I have compassion on the crowd, because they have been with me now three days and have nothing to eat. And if I send them away hungry to their homes, they will faint on the way. And some of them have come from far away." And his disciples answered him, "How can one feed these people with bread here in this desolate place?" And he asked them, "How many loaves do you have?" They said, "Seven." And he directed the crowd to sit down on the ground. And he took the seven loaves, and having given thanks, he broke them and gave them to his disciples to set before the people; and they set them before the crowd. And they had a few small fish. And having blessed them, he said that these also should be set before them. And they ate and were satisfied. And they took up the broken pieces left over, seven baskets full. And there were about four thousand people. And he sent them away. And immediately he got into the boat with his disciples and went to the district of Dalmanutha.

Consider This

The centrality of eating in the Bible cannot be overemphasized. The great grace in the garden of Eden was that the man and woman could eat from any tree in the garden save one. Consequently, the great fall from grace surrounded eating. At the end of all things broken and the beginning of all things made new, we will enjoy a grand wedding feast—the wedding feast of the Lamb.

Eating can be a great blessing and it can be a great curse. Most of us know both realities all too well. Perhaps this is also part of the reason fasting is so essential to growing as a disciple of Jesus. Feasting is a blessing he gives to us. Might fasting be a blessing we give to him?

Eating was central in the ministry of Jesus. In today's text, he fed thousands of Gentiles with a few fish and several loaves of bread. A couple of chapters back he fed thousands of Jews, again with a few fish and loaves of bread.

When it came to food he took scarce resources and transformed them into abundant provisions. Remember in that first feeding miracle he said to his disciples, "You give them something to eat." Giving people something to eat may be all at once the most practical, compassionate, and loving thing a person can do for another.

It makes me think about my mother. She loves giving people something to eat, and she's quite good at it. It makes me think about Chick-fil-A and the sign on the wall of all their restaurants quoting their founder, Truett Cathey: "Food is essential to life, therefore make it good." Chick-fil-A is the only fast food restaurant chain in the world that has managed to make feeding people, and all the thoughtful touches of service that accompany it, a true ministry.

It's tempting to take this in a spiritual direction and talk about how Jesus feeds us with something far more than food. While this is true, let us not forget the inextricable connection of eating and drinking—bread and wine—as the definitive sign of our relationship with him. The gospel is all wrapped up in eating.

Finally, let's remember that final conversation with Peter on the shore of the Sea of Galilee when Jesus asked him, "Peter, do you love me?" In reply to Peter's yes, Jesus commanded, "Feed my sheep" (see John 21:15).

We are told at the final judgment that one of the greatest ways we have of encountering Jesus on earth is through the presence of people who hunger. On that day he will say to the people on his right, the sheep, "I was hungry and you gave me something to eat" (Matt. 25:35).

Given all of this, let's be very mindful of the constant opportunities we have to obey Jesus in the most practical every day of ways—feeding others.

Take someone to lunch today and take lunch to someone tomorrow. The Holy Spirit loves to work through food! Thank God!

The Prayer

Spirit of the living God, fall afresh on me.

The Questions

- Why do we tend to separate physical things from spiritual things?
- What does Jesus teach us on this account?

On the Difference between Faith and Risk Management

42

MARK 8:11–21 NRSV | The Pharisees came and began to argue with him, asking him for a sign from heaven, to test him. And he sighed deeply in his spirit and said, "Why does this generation ask for a sign? Truly I tell you, no sign will be given to this generation." And he left them, and getting into the boat again, he went across to the other side.

Now the disciples had forgotten to bring any bread; and they had only one loaf with them in the boat. And he cautioned

Yeast is a leaven that spread quickly through the flour.

The underlying reason for the Pharisees + Herod was to kill Jesus — They spread their evil

them, saying, "Watch out—beware of the yeast of the Pharisees and the yeast of Herod." They said to one another, "It is because we have no bread." And becoming aware of it, Jesus said to them, "Why are you talking about having no bread? Do you still not perceive or understand? Are your hearts hardened? Do you have eyes, and fail to see? Do you have ears, and fail to hear? And do you not remember? When I broke the five loaves for the five thousand, how many baskets full of broken pieces did you collect?" They said to him, "Twelve." "And the seven for the four thousand, how many baskets full of broken pieces did you collect?" And they said to him, "Seven." Then he said to them, "Do you not yet understand?"

Consider This

We want signs. That's where Satan began with Jesus. Remember back in the wilderness after Jesus fasted forty days when Satan approached him with this, "If you are the Son of God, turn these stones to bread." Jesus promptly turned that one around with the reply, "Man does not live by bread alone but by every word that comes from the mouth of God" (see Matthew 4).

If we are honest, we want a sign. We need to see something before we believe. Jesus says it's just the opposite. Those who believe will see. Faith is a disposition of the heart—eyes that see and ears that hear. Jesus warned them—demanding signs is the antithesis of faith. Faith is not an empirical certainty but a deep inner confidence. The clamor for certainty leavens the clarity of faith.

Now the disciples had forgotten to bring any bread; and they had only one loaf with them in the boat. And he cautioned them, saying, "Watch out—beware of the yeast of the Pharisees and the yeast of Herod."

So often we come to big decisions in life and rather than the way of faith, we opt for the path of certainty. We list the pros and cons and do the cost-benefit analysis, hoping the defining sign will present itself. And to be sure, due diligence in our decision-making can be a good thing, but I'm not sure it's the way of faith. I have a hunch that faith is built more on counting the cost than analyzing the data.

Are you facing a big decision in the days ahead? Ask yourself, what would it mean to walk by faith and not by sight? Faith is not blind. It's a much deeper, richer, and ultimately clearer way of seeing. Spend more time counting the cost of the decision rather than endlessly seeking more data. Don't let the quest for certainty override the gift of clarity. The ways of the Pharisees, which is the religious version of the ways of the world, leaven faith by amplifying the fear of failure. Faith means risk, not risk-management.

The Prayer
Spirit of the living God, fall afresh on me.

The Questions
- What keeps you from walking by faith? Fear of failure? Looking foolish? Indifference?
- What might a practical step of real faith look like in your life right now?

43 Why Miracles Will Never Be Enough

MARK 8:22–26 | They came to Bethsaida, and some people brought a blind man and begged Jesus to touch him. He took the blind man by the hand and led him outside the village. When he had spit on the man's eyes and put his hands on him, Jesus asked, "Do you see anything?"

He looked up and said, "I see people; they look like trees walking around."

Once more Jesus put his hands on the man's eyes. Then his eyes were opened, his sight was restored, and he saw everything clearly. Jesus sent him home, saying, "Don't even go into the village."

Consider This

Do you remember how the Gospel of Mark began? "The beginning of the good news about Jesus the Messiah, the Son of God, as it is written in Isaiah the prophet" (1:1–2).

Mark began with Isaiah. And the truth is, he never left Isaiah. Isaiah's prophecy about the coming of the kingdom of God has been the quiet subtext running behind the whole gospel so far.

Do you remember Jesus' first sermon, the nineteen-word manifesto of a message? "The time has come," he said. "The kingdom of God has come near. Repent and believe the good news!" (Mark 1:15).

From that beginning, Jesus has moved about the country-side demonstrating the nearness of the kingdom. We need to stay in touch with this bigger picture. When the kingdom of God breaks in it reverses the kingdom of the world. Let's recall more of Isaiah's prophecy concerning the kingdom. Watch for the predicted reversals that signify its coming.

> Then will the eyes of the blind be opened
> and the ears of the deaf unstopped.
> Then will the lame leap like a deer,
> and the mute tongue shout for joy.
> Water will gush forth in the wilderness
> and streams in the desert.
> The burning sand will become a pool,
> the thirsty ground bubbling springs.
> In the haunts where jackals once lay,
> grass and reeds and papyrus will grow. (Isa. 35:5–7)

It brings us to today's text. But before we go there, let's remember when Jesus opened the ears of a deaf man and restored his inability to speak. In this text, he opens the eyes of a blind man. Jesus is turning everything around. Remember the paralytic man who was lowered through the roof of the house? Jesus told him to rise up, take up his mat, and walk, and he did.

Eyes of the blind opened? Check! Ears of the deaf unstopped? Check! Lame leaping like a deer? Check! Mute tongue shouting for joy? Check!

It sounds strange to say, but it's all too easy to get caught up in the demonstrations and miss the bigger reality being demonstrated. I think for Jesus, at times the miracles actually got in the way of his larger mission. It's why he wanted to keep a lot of that discreet. People needed help and he was moved with compassion to help them. However, he knew people needed more help than a mere miracle. People most need the reversal of everything broken and the restoration of everything made new. People most need the world to be restored to the original intent of its Creator.

The same is true in our own lives. We need the help of God desperately in so many situations. We need miracles. But more than help for our particular situations, we need the reign and rule of the God of heaven and earth to be completely reinstated everywhere. When this happens, there will be no more tears and no more sin and no more death. There will be no more need for miracles. This is the bigger picture and the better horizon we must constantly lift our eyes to perceive.

It's why the prayer of all prayers is not "Give us this day, our daily bread," but "Thy Kingdom come. Thy will be done, on earth as it is in heaven." Yes, we must feed the hungry, but we labor and pray for the day when there will be no more hunger. Do we believe this?

The thing signified is always more important than the signs pointing to it. Miracles are short-term solutions, but they point to the long-term reality. That's what we need to remember. Let's keep that in perspective.

The Prayer

Spirit of the living God, fall afresh on me.

The Questions

- What might it look like for our ambitions and our prayers and actions to become more captivated by the bigger picture and the further horizon of the movement of God's kingdom and less attached to the consuming challenges of right now?
- How might that kind of shift change the present moment?

The Concerns of God

44

MARK 8:27–33 ESV | And Jesus went on with his disciples to the villages of Caesarea Philippi. And on the way he asked his disciples, "Who do people say that I am?" And they told him, "John the Baptist; and others say, Elijah; and others, one of the prophets." And he asked them, "But who do you say that I am?" Peter answered him, "You are the Christ." And he strictly charged them to tell no one about him.

And he began to teach them that the Son of Man must suffer many things and be rejected by the elders and the chief priests and the scribes and be killed, and after three days rise again. And he said this plainly. And Peter took him aside and began to rebuke him. But turning and seeing his disciples, he rebuked Peter and said, "Get behind me, Satan! For you are not setting your mind on the things of God, but on the things of man."

Consider This

There are human concerns and then there are the concerns of God. We humans are concerned about so many things and surely God must be concerned with some of the things that concern us. I suspect, however, that God is not concerned with many of the things that concern us. In fact, many things we concern ourselves with can choke out the life of God in us. Remember the parable of the sower and the seed that fell in the thorny ground?

> "And others are those sown among the thorns: these are the ones who hear the word, but the cares of the world, and the lure of wealth, and the desire for other things come in and choke the word, and it yields nothing." (Mark 4:18–19 NRSV)

The opening scripture sheds some light on at least a couple of the concerns of God. First, God is concerned with our knowing Jesus Christ and who he is. He wants us to get it not like an answer on a test but as a deeply personal relationship. "You are the Messiah." It's one thing to say Jesus is God, which is accurate. It takes it a step further to say God is Jesus.

Second, he wants us to get the way God works and accomplishes his purposes in the world. Remember Isaiah—the text running alongside Mark's storytelling? Isaiah put it this way:

> For my thoughts are not your thoughts, nor are your ways my ways, says the LORD. For as the heavens are higher than the earth, so are my ways higher than your ways and my thoughts than your thoughts. (Isa. 55:8–9 NRSV)

Peter was not thinking this way. He was holding on to the Israeli dream—the restoration of the kingdom to Israel. Because he thought he knew how the future should unfold and the role Jesus would play, he tried to veto the plan Jesus put forward. Jesus responded pretty sternly, *"Get behind me, Satan! For you are not setting your mind on the things of God, but on the things of man."*

The plans of God will often make no sense to us. And the more confident we are in our own conflicting plans the more absurd it will feel. My own life bears this out in a small way. I spent the better part of a decade preparing for a career in public service. I earned degrees in public administration and law, passed the bar exam, and went to work. I served on the staff of then Senator David Pryor in Washington D.C. Then the itinerary changed. I began to discern a calling to full-time work in the church. I was not having it! I suspect my early reactions to this change in direction had something of the effect of rebuking Jesus. I'm still learning along the way the meaning of saying, "You are the Messiah." It's another way of saying yours is the kingdom. It's shorthand for, "your way is higher, better, and truer." To say, "You are the Messiah," means saying something like, "I am no longer my own but yours." It's the ultimate pledge of trust and promise of obedience. It means to trust that the concerns of God also include God's concern for me. "You are the Messiah." It must come to mean more every time we say it. Let that be our concern today.

The Prayer
Spirit of the living God, fall afresh on me.

The Questions
- Where are you in the journey of moving from Jesus is the Messiah to Jesus is my Lord? What is the next step?

45 The Problem with Lowest Common Denominator Discipleship

MARK 8:34–38 NRSV | He called the crowd with his disciples, and said to them, "If any want to become my followers, let them deny themselves and take up their cross and follow me.

For those who want to save their life will lose it, and those who lose their life for my sake, and for the sake of the gospel, will save it. For what will it profit them to gain the whole world and forfeit their life? Indeed, what can they give in return for their life? Those who are ashamed of me and of my words in this adulterous and sinful generation, of them the Son of Man will also be ashamed when he comes in the glory of his Father with the holy angels."

Consider This

Note how Mark carefully points out that Jesus *called the crowd with his disciples*. This makes abundantly clear Jesus' intention to make this bold call to discipleship well beyond his initial disciples.

This is a very challenging teaching and, yet, in twenty-first-century Christianity, it has become so challenge-by-choice optional. I mean, Jesus didn't intend this for everyone, did he? Can't I just believe in Jesus and everything will turn out okay? What's this about carrying a Roman cross and letting my own life go to follow Jesus? It sounds so extreme and hard. Surely this can't be what he meant.

The gospel is a radical solution to a catastrophic problem. Imagine if you had terminal cancer and the doctor told you all you needed to do was to believe in the efficacy of the treatment. You didn't actually have to take the treatment—just believe in it. It's absurd. You would go to your grave believing in the treatment, yet never having actually been treated.

I think this is the case with so much Christianity over the past one hundred years or so. We've wanted to reduce it to its lowest possible threshold to the point where we simply want to know if you have made a decision. Trusting Jesus is not a transaction. It is a totalizing abandonment of oneself to God. It is the shifting of the center of gravity from self-determination to revolving all of life around God and his kingdom. Where did we ever get the idea that believing something in your head or saying that you believe in the truth of something could somehow add up to following Jesus? Jesus put it this way: *"For whoever wants to save their life will lose it, but whoever loses their life for me and for the gospel will save it"* (Mark 8:35).

Do we really believe this is true? Spend some time going over those twenty-four words today.

The Prayer

Spirit of the living God, fall afresh on me.

The Questions

- Why are you following Jesus?

To follow Jesus you give up the old us and say if me & what do what God want—

Seeing behind the Curtain vs. Beholding through the Veil

46

MARK 9:1–13 | And he said to them, "Truly I tell you, some who are standing here will not taste death before they see that the kingdom of God has come with power."

After six days Jesus took Peter, James and John with him and led them up a high mountain, where they were all alone. There he was transfigured before them. His clothes became dazzling white, whiter than anyone in the world could bleach them. And there appeared before them Elijah and Moses, who were talking with Jesus.

Peter said to Jesus, "Rabbi, it is good for us to be here. Let us put up three shelters—one for you, one for Moses and one for Elijah." (He did not know what to say, they were so frightened.)

Then a cloud appeared and covered them, and a voice came from the cloud: "This is my Son, whom I love. Listen to him!"

Suddenly, when they looked around, they no longer saw anyone with them except Jesus.

As they were coming down the mountain, Jesus gave them orders not to tell anyone what they had seen until the Son of Man had risen from the dead. They kept the matter to themselves, discussing what "rising from the dead" meant.

And they asked him, "Why do the teachers of the law say that Elijah must come first?" *John the Baptist*

Jesus replied, "To be sure, Elijah does come first, and restores all things. Why then is it written that the Son of Man must suffer much and be rejected? But I tell you, Elijah has come, and they have done to him everything they wished, just as it is written about him."

Consider This

There are two ways of getting a behind-the-scenes look at something. There's seeing behind the curtain and there's seeing through the veil.

My friend and colleague Andy Miller, who is Seedbed's director of publishing, gave me a behind-the-scenes tour of the Franklin First Methodist Church's new church campus construction project. I had driven by there countless times and watched as the beautiful structure had risen up from the ground, but I had never been inside. As we walked along, I could clearly see the emerging floor plan with tons of steel framing rooms and spaces of various sizes. Wires ran into and out of everywhere. I could begin to imagine what this majestic place would look like in the future. Andy had lived with the vision so intimately that he could practically see it and it came through in his vivid tour guidance. I was being privileged to see a work in progress behind the veil.

Recently on a work trip to the campus of Asbury Theological Seminary, where I have served for the past fifteen years, I experienced something of a seeing behind the veil on a building project. Rather than staying in the Asbury Inn campus hotel, they put me in a nearby dormitory known as the William House. I had been in there probably a hundred times over the years. I knew all the curried smells of international student home cooking. I knew the messiness of all the lived-in spaces with the carpet stains and tears from all the efforts to make a dorm room seem new by rearranging the furnishings. As I walked to the front door, everything looked like it had always looked, but as I passed through the front door and into my room everything had changed. I felt like I was in a brand-new Embassy Suites Hotel. The place had been completely remodeled and I was being privileged to a behind-the-curtain experience of this new-old place.

These two scenes serve as apt metaphors for the nature of our lives. There is the outer appearance and there is an inner reality. Sometimes the outer appearance looks new and shiny and the inner reality is somewhere in the process of catching up. Other times, the outer appearance may have the same worn look as always, but the inside radiates with a total makeover. Both scenes offer us an analogous picture of what transformation looks like in various stages of progress. The Bible calls this "sanctification."

We tend to spend a lot of time in life on the outer appearance only to realize as life progresses there's only so much we can do with it. Somewhere along the way we hopefully abandon cosmetic improvements to awaken to the inside project, where no matter how old the outer structure, the inward reality can become utterly and completely transformed.

None of this, however, describes the scene in today's text. Transfiguration is to transformation as Jesus is to Peter. The transfiguration takes us up on a high mountain where we are privileged to see through the veil where we behold the almost indescribable reality of ultimate reality. This is neither a vision nor a dream. It is neither a glimpse of the future nor a remembrance of the past.

Standing in the presence of Jesus with Peter, James, and John, we behold the mysterious convergence of our storied past and our transfigured future in the present moment of the presence of God. We hear from the Father, behold the glory of the eternal Son, and breathe in the breath of the Holy Spirit.

We are glimpsing the timelessness of eternity breaking in on the present time. On that mountain, we are seeing through the veil that separates heaven and earth and glimpsing the kingdom of God in all its glorious indescribable essence— bright shining as the sun.

This is the glorious end of all of the sanctifying grace of God, which is itself only the beginning of the unfathomable reality of "Your Kingdom come, your will be done, on earth as it is in heaven." On that mountain, we behold the life, everlasting in quality and quantity, for which we were made; the beloved community of all who have followed Jesus before us and who will come behind us together in the resplendent presence of the beloved God of all glory.

The justifying grace of salvation is the door. The sanctifying grace of transformation is the process. The perfecting grace of transfiguration is the end. The only way there is through the cross of Jesus, apart from whom we have no hope of finding it. The cross is the only cure for the terminal cancer of sin and death, but it has a 100 percent cure rate.

And this reality we refer to as the Mount of Transfiguration? It is as real and present right now as it was on the day described in the Scriptures. This is not some distant ethereal future to which we will one day fly away. No, this is the reality just through the veil. This is not a distant reality we hope in. It is the present reality we hope from.

> We know that the whole creation has been groaning as in the pains of childbirth right up to the present time. (Rom. 8:22)

The point of this text is not that we would clamor for this Mount of Transfiguration experience to happen again and this time for us. The point is for us to realize that what happened that day as we have it in Scripture, happened to and for us. Because we were there, we are there. This is not about mystical perception but concrete reality. May the Holy Spirit order our understanding and experience of the Word of God accordingly.

To my scholarly minded friends—please do not interpret me as propagating some version of a post-millennial realized eschatology. I am speaking of the transfiguration as a perfect glimpse through the veil into the kingdom of God—which exists gloriously already and yet remains unquestionably not yet. *And he said to them, "Truly I tell you, some who are standing here will not taste death before they see that the kingdom of God has come with power."*

The Prayer

Spirit of the living God, fall afresh on me.

The Questions

- What about the transfiguration blows your mind the most?
- Is there a fresh takeaway for you?

47 What to Do in the Face of a Discipleship Fail

MARK 9:14–20 ESV | And when they came to the disciples, they saw a great crowd around them, and scribes arguing with them. And immediately all the crowd, when they saw him, were greatly amazed and ran up to him and greeted him. And he asked them, "What are you arguing about with them?" And someone from the crowd answered him, "Teacher, I brought my son to you, for he has a spirit that makes him mute. And whenever it seizes him, it throws him down, and he foams and grinds his teeth and becomes rigid. So I asked your disciples to cast it out, and they were not able." And he answered them, "O faithless generation, how long am I to be with you? How long am I to bear with you? Bring him to me." And they brought the boy to him. And when the spirit saw him, immediately it convulsed the boy, and he fell on the ground and rolled about, foaming at the mouth.

Consider This

Transfiguration one day and trouble the next. Life ever moves from mountain-top experiences to chaotic messes in the valleys, even for Jesus. Why should it be different for us.

Understand the situation here. Jesus left the nine disciples for a short time away. While he was gone, the Feds showed up on their gotcha campaign to continue their investigation into this exciting upstart movement afoot in Galilee. The pressure was on, and what came forward but another impossible situation. Could these disciples get it done? No. In the wake of their failure, the religious officials pounced and an argument broke out.

This is a classic picture of everyday life. The powers of darkness meet up with the presence of God in the midst of human pain and all of this inside a larger context of conflict. This is what the powers of darkness do. They foment chaos, confusion, and conflict while exploiting peoples' problems and amplifying their pain. Multiply this by a few hundred million and you get a pretty good picture of the world we live in. Transfiguration mountains are the exception on the still-broken side of the not-yet kingdom. Still, we must be good news people at work in the midst of what is so often a very bad news situation.

It's just so easy to become pessimistic, because we know all too well the situation of the disciples who couldn't quite get it done. In the face of so much unresolved pain and unhealed suffering, it's all too easy to slip into pessimistic attitudes and cynical spirits. We must rebuke these responses in ourselves the minute we detect them rising up because they are toxic to faith.

So how does faith respond in the face of failure? While we know pessimism isn't the answer, neither is optimism. In between those poles lives perhaps the worst response of all: a defeated spirit of resignation.

Here's my prescription in the face of this kind of failure: (1) Learn from Jesus in the face of failure. Tomorrow he will teach us something about this situation. (2) Get back up and get on the horse again. Failure is going to happen. We don't have to accept failure but neither do we need to be surprised by it. It's the nature of the game when you are dealing with rogue satanic forces. Jesus is going to win the war, but the troops are going to lose some battles along the way. There will be discipleship fails. The team will lose some contests. Faith forges on in the face of failure wiser for the battles ahead.

Let failure take its toll on our self-confidence because what we need more is God confidence. When self-confidence fails, it gives rise to humility, and when God confidence rises, boldness is born. This is precisely the posture of discipleship Jesus wants for his disciples: humble boldness. It's the powerfully beautiful convergence of poverty of spirit, meekness, and purity of heart. This is a learned disposition only

Jesus can teach us, and once we learn it, we will realize only the Holy Spirit can empower its implementation in our lives.

The Prayer

Spirit of the living God, fall afresh on me.

The Questions

- Where do you find yourself failing in your discipleship at the moment?

The Problem with Lazy Faith and the Way beyond It

48

MARK 9:21–29 NRSV | Jesus asked the father, "How long has this been happening to him?" And he said, "From childhood. It has often cast him into the fire and into the water, to destroy him; but if you are able to do anything, have pity on us and help us." Jesus said to him, "If you are able!—All things can be done for the one who believes." Immediately the father of the child cried out, "I believe; help my unbelief!" When Jesus saw that a crowd came running together, he rebuked the unclean spirit, saying to it, "You spirit that keeps this boy from speaking and hearing, I command you, come out of him, and never enter him again!" After crying out and convulsing him terribly, it came out, and the boy was like a corpse, so that most of them said, "He is dead." But Jesus took him by the hand and lifted him up, and he was able to stand. When he had entered the house, his disciples asked him privately, "Why could we not cast it out?" He said to them, "This kind can come out only through prayer."

Consider This

"How long has this been happening to him?"

The question reveals the nature of God, who cares deeply about human brokenness. It's not something he needed to know in order to heal the boy. He wanted to know because he cared.

"but if you are able to do anything, have pity on us and help us."

We know the man had faith because he brought his son to Jesus' disciples for help. As we discussed earlier, they failed in their efforts. It's perhaps an obvious observation, but definitely worth noting here that because of the failure of Jesus' disciples, the man had lost faith in Jesus. Of all the things one might say to Jesus, it's hard to imagine speaking these four words: "If you are able . . ."

Don't you love Jesus' response?

"If you are able!—All things can be done for the one who believes."

It's sort of like he's saying, "You've got to be kidding me! Did you really just question if I was able to cast out this spirit?" Jesus seems to be growing weary of the lack of faith he finds among the race of men. Remember his lament from the previous text? "O faithless generation, how long am I to be with you? How long am I to bear with you?" This would not be a good thing to hear from the Son of God. I suspect, though, he might say a similar thing to our generation. Sadly, it probably characterizes most generations. The last thing I want to hear Jesus say about me would be this one word: "unbelieving." The good news is the gospel word Jesus speaks into every person of every generation: *"All things can be done for the one who believes."* Faith is the fruit of divine revelation wherein the Holy Spirit works in the human heart to convince one of a reality that could not otherwise be whole heartedly embraced.

The father responds with one of the most classic lines in the New Testament, *"I believe; help my unbelief!"*

With this prayer, the father gave us the gift of piercing honesty and, if we are honest, we know exactly what he meant. We are all a messy mixture of belief and unbelief, of faith and doubt. It's all too easy to simply accept this reality and resign ourselves to it. After all, we're human, right? And Jesus was human. Jesus waits for a generation who will not be content to live out their lives in the lazy place between belief and unbelief. Sure, it's an unreasonable expectation given the immensity of impossibility constantly surrounding us. Still, he longs to see it in us.

We know what happened next. Jesus cast out the evil spirit and, if that weren't enough, he raised the boy from the dead immediately following. We need scenes like this emblazoned on our imagination. In fact, this is one of the reasons for reading the Gospels over and over and over again, so these stories will become fused in our memory.

My keen interest, however, is in the exchange between Jesus and his disciples later that day.

When he had entered the house, his disciples asked him privately, "Why could we not cast it out?" He said to them, "This kind can come out only through prayer."

So did the disciples forget to pray before they tried casting out the evil spirit? I don't think so. I'm sure they prayed. They probably prayed in Jesus' name. I think the problem is the disciples lived in the same place as the boy's father—somewhere between belief and unbelief. I don't think Jesus was talking about prayer as a practice or technique here. I think he meant something much larger than a simple act of speaking to God on behalf of people in need. In my humble opinion, when Jesus references prayer here, he's talking about a totalizing way of life, a way of living in the kind of faith that excludes unbelief. It reminds me of something Henri Nouwen wrote years ago that I've never forgotten:

> The word "prayer" stands for a radical interruption of the vicious chain of interlocking dependencies leading to violence and war and for an entering into a totally new dwelling place. It points to a new way of speaking, a new way of breathing, a new way of being together, a new way of knowing, yes, a whole new way of living. . . . Prayer is the center of the Christian life. *It is the only necessary thing.* (Luke 10:42)[5]

---

5. Henri Nouwen, "Prayer and Peacemaking," *The Only Necessary Thing: Living a Prayerful Life* (New York: Crossroad Publishing, 1999), 25.

The Prayer

Spirit of the living God, fall afresh on me.

The Questions

- What will it take for you to become brutally honest about your unbelief?
- What is underneath this unbelief for you? *Superficial Belief*

Why We Aren't the Champions

49

MARK 9:30–37 | They left that place and passed through Galilee. Jesus did not want anyone to know where they were, because he was teaching his disciples. He said to them, "The Son of Man is going to be delivered into the hands of men. They will kill him, and after three days he will rise." But they did not understand what he meant and were afraid to ask him about it.

They came to Capernaum. When he was in the house, he asked them, "What were you arguing about on the road?" But they kept quiet because on the way they had argued about who was the greatest.

Sitting down, Jesus called the Twelve and said, "Anyone who wants to be first must be the very last, and the servant of all."

He took a little child whom he placed among them. Taking the child in his arms, he said to them, "Whoever welcomes one of these little children in my name welcomes me; and whoever welcomes me does not welcome me but the one who sent me."

God

Consider This

"I'm the greatest." Who says that? Okay, well there was Muhammad Ali who gave himself the nickname, "The Greatest," but it's just not something you hear people saying too often.

Until we realize the sin du jour of every age is that of comparing ourselves to others. Every comparison we make with another person, whether we admit it or not, results in one who is greater and one who is lesser.

It's human nature to want to be the greatest, to be the best, to be number one. That the disciples argued about who was the greatest as they walked along the road was par for the course then as well as today.

A sports team can be ranked at the bottom of the league, but if they happen to pull off a win, all of a sudden the index fingers shoot up into the air of players and fans alike accompanied by the exultant cries, "We're number one!"

We all do it. It's why one of the favorite songs of all time has to be Queen's "We Are the Champions." I suppose a little friendly competition can be a good thing, if only we could leave it on the field. Unfortunately, we can't, or at least we don't. Oftentimes, as I'm scrolling through Facebook or Instagram, it strikes me as one massive competition to show who has the most perfect kids and the most awesome family vacations and the most dreamy homes and meals and on it goes. The competition really kicks into high gear as December rolls around and the dreaded Christmas letters start pouring in. You know what I'm talking about. Someday I'm going to write a Christmas letter that tells all the horror stories and dark secrets of the prior year's real family life. Imagine reading that one.

Jesus takes this mentality and turns it upside down. He does it by redefining the meaning of the word "greatness." Greatness, according to God, has nothing to do with being superior and everything to do with becoming a servant. It doesn't mean making oneself a doormat for others to walk on. Servanthood does not mean thinking of yourself as a loser or as somehow worse than others. It means putting the needs of others ahead of yourself. This is hard, and if it seems easy you are either not actually doing it, or maturing into a bona fide follower of Jesus.

A final note: While serving means activity, in the greater sense it means identity. This is why Jesus lifts up the child in their midst. A child is a child not because of some effort they make. It is who they are. In those days, a child was as status-less as a slave. To be a servant is a mentality. It is a state of mind. Paul put it like this:

> In your relationships with one another, have the same mindset as Christ Jesus: Who, being in very nature God, did not consider equality with God something to be used to his own advantage; rather, he made himself nothing by taking the very nature of a servant. (Phil. 2:5–7)

Becoming a servant is a way of seeing oneself in a new light, in the light of the greater greatness of the glory of God. In the end, becoming a servant is a way of seeing others in a new light, in the light of the greater love of the love God.

The Prayer

Spirit of the living God, fall afresh on me.

The Questions

- It is one thing to serve, yet another to take on the mentality of a servant. How are you doing this in your life?

50 How Sin Continues to Win and How to Beat It

MARK 9:38–50 ESV | John said to him, "Teacher, we saw someone casting out demons in your name, and we tried to stop him, because he was not following us." But Jesus said, "Do not stop him, for no one who does a mighty work in my name will be able soon afterward to speak evil of me. For the one who is not against us is for us. For truly, I say to you, whoever gives you a cup of water to drink because you belong to Christ will by no means lose his reward.

"Whoever causes one of these little ones who believe in me to sin, it would be better for him if a great millstone were hung around his neck and he were thrown into the sea. And if your hand causes you to sin, cut it off. It is better for you to enter life crippled than with two hands to go to hell, to the unquenchable fire. And if your foot causes you to sin, cut it off. It is better for you to enter life lame than with two feet to be thrown into hell. And if your eye causes you to sin, tear it out. It is better for you to enter the kingdom of God with one eye than with two eyes to be thrown into hell, 'where their worm does not die and the fire is not quenched.' For everyone will be salted with fire. Salt is good, but if the salt has lost its saltiness, how will you make it salty again? Have salt in yourselves, and be at peace with one another."

Consider This

There's too much going on in this text to adequately cover it in this brief venue. I'll choose one topic: sin.

Jesus' message is as stark as it is simple and can be brought down to three words: sin is deadly.

On the one hand, Jesus employs the use of hyperbole, yet on the other, he does not overstate his case. Sin means death. Sin doesn't kill with the surgical strike of a bullet, but like the slow cell-scorching scourge of cancer.

It reminds me of the more modern-day stories that get passed along to describe sin. There's the story of how monkeys are caught in certain parts of the world. Trappers cut a small hole into a hollow gourd and fill it with the monkey equivalent of candy bars. The monkey reaches into the gourd, gets a handful of the treats, and when he tries to pull his hand out, the hole is not large enough for his fist to fit through. The only thing between the monkey and freedom is his grip on the candy. He ultimately succumbs to the trap.

Then there's the story of how wolves are trapped in certain parts of Alaska. They bury a very sharp knife down into the ice with only the tip of the blade exposed. On top of the blade they place a large hunk of raw meat. The wolf begins eating the meat and, in the process, cuts his tongue. Unable to distinguish the blood from the raw meat and the blood from his tongue, the wolf bleeds to death in the process of enjoying his last meal.

Of all the stories I've told my kids, they seem to remember these the most. They can tell these stories in striking detail. We get it. We understand what sin is and what it does and yet we still do it. Even the most dire warnings don't manage to steer us clear of the seduction of sin. Jesus wants us to imagine taking a hatchet and hacking off our hand if it leads us into sin. Think about that. Jesus goes to such lengths because sin is so deadly. He's saying it would be better for you to endure the pain of amputation than the outcome of a tortured life of sin.

Maybe there's another obvious message hiding within Jesus' stern warning. What if he's calling us to preemptive strategies as relates to sin abatement? Because of Jesus' death on the cross, sin has lost its power over us. Yet somehow it remains powerful. Permit me to be frank. Whether it be the sins of pride or gluttony or lust or envy or fill in the blank, sin continues to win in our lives because we have adopted a strategy of management instead of eradication. We choose sin-management because we aren't willing to do what sin-eradication requires. Even worse, we deem the eradication of sin impossible. So what does sin-eradication require?

It takes more than me and the Holy Spirit. It requires other people. Until I'm ready to let a couple of other people into the inner sanctum of my soul to help me overcome sin, it won't happen.

The Prayer

Spirit of the living God, fall afresh on me.

The Questions

- What's your mentality with respect to sin: management or eradication? If you could eradicate one sin in your life, which one would it be?

On the Reason for Marriage and the Difficulty of Divorce

51

MARK 10:1–12 NRSV | He left that place and went to the region of Judea and beyond the Jordan. And crowds again gathered around him; and, as was his custom, he again taught them.

Some Pharisees came, and to test him they asked, "Is it lawful for a man to divorce his wife?" He answered them, "What did

Moses command you?" They said, "Moses allowed a man to write a certificate of dismissal and to divorce her." But Jesus said to them, "Because of your hardness of heart he wrote this commandment for you. But from the beginning of creation, 'God made them male and female.' 'For this reason a man shall leave his father and mother and be joined to his wife, and the two shall become one flesh.' So they are no longer two, but one flesh. Therefore what God has joined together, let no one separate."

Then in the house the disciples asked him again about this matter. He said to them, "Whoever divorces his wife and marries another commits adultery against her; and if she divorces her husband and marries another, she commits adultery."

Consider This

In this text, Jesus continues his journey to Jerusalem. He's teaching along the way when a group of Pharisees approach him with this question: *"Is it lawful for a man to divorce his wife?"*

They put Jesus on the spot, attempting to get him to position himself. Remember John, that prophet who lost his head over his conviction about marriage and divorce? It looks like the Pharisees are trying to get Jesus caught up in that controversy; maybe there's another beheading service just around the corner.

Jesus lays a bit of a trap for his trappers.

"What did Moses command you?"

They said, "Moses allowed a man to write a certificate of dismissal and to divorce her."

Now that Deuteronomy 24:1 is in play, Jesus takes them to school with his skills of interpreting Scripture by Scripture. He's not going to go tit-for-tat, litigating Mosaic law. No, Jesus goes for the proverbial jugular, turning all the way back to Scroll #1 and creation (i.e., Genesis 1:27–28 and 2:24).

"Because of your hardness of heart he wrote this commandment for you. But from the beginning of creation, 'God made them male and female.' 'For this reason a man shall leave his father and mother and be joined to his wife, and the two shall become one flesh.' So they are no longer two, but one flesh. Therefore what God has joined together, let no one separate."

Did you note that move from the letter of the Law to the spirit behind it; that bit about hard-heartedness? Divorce is not the creational intention of God. The Law made allowance for it via post-Eden legislation and mostly as a measure of protection for women, but divorce is never God's best.

Many reading along today have likely been through a divorce and, in most cases, they could reference the inevitability of irreconcilability. Just as divorce was never God's intention, no one who has been divorced would claim it was ever their intention. In a broken world, things break despite our best intentions and efforts. For those who have been divorced, you need not live under condemnation but in Christ, where condemnation has been crucified. Our God brings beauty from ashes and new beginnings from broken promises.

repentance

(Permit me a pastoral word of caution: while reconciliation of a marriage may not have been possible, working through forgiveness is essential. Remember, unforgiveness is akin to drinking poison and expecting it to kill the other person.)

For those reading along who may be in a difficult moment of marriage, let me offer these words of grace. Marriage between a man and a woman is God's creational intent for those who he calls to marry. The covenant of marriage, which is a fiery hot crucible, is designed to withstand all the chaos human brokenness can bring. Given time and patience and the abiding presence of the Holy Spirit, nothing is impossible with God. The chaos of conflict can only be reconciled at the foot of the cross.

A learned woman once remarked to me that there were four movements of the transforming grace of God. 1. Justification. 2. Sanctification. 3. Marriage. 4. Children.

Another learned man put it like this: "Love is blind, but marriage is an eye-opener."

Back in the days before he married, my friend Chris Tomlin recounted to me a conversation he had with Steven Curtis Chapman about marriage. Chapman said to Chris, "Can I tell you what marriage is? Marriage is when God gets your life on an anvil and beats the #@%* out of you."

I love how Jesus picks up the language of "Because . . ." Only he doesn't explicitly identify the reason. My take? Marriage, like no other institution on earth, holds the capacity to reveal the glory of God through the practice of suffering love.

Note: Persons suffering in an abusive marriage may find the concept of "suffering love" particularly unhelpful. If you find yourself in an abusive marital relationship, all bets are off. Seek help. Take refuge. As hard as it may seem, extricate yourself from the situation. There are many resources available to help in such situations.

The Prayer

Spirit of the living God, fall afresh on me.

The Questions

- Can you think of a marriage where you have witnessed the glory of God manifested?

The Big Problem of the Powerful

52

MARK 10:13–16 | People were bringing little children to Jesus for him to place his hands on them, but the disciples rebuked them. When Jesus saw this, he was indignant. He said to them, "Let the little children come to me, and do not hinder them, for the kingdom of God belongs to such as these. Truly I tell you, anyone who will not receive the kingdom of God like a little child will never enter it." And he took the children in his arms, placed his hands on them and blessed them.

Consider This

I've got to be honest, when I read this passage, images of the children's sermon come to mind. I hear a church congregation singing, "Tell me the stories of Jesus I love to hear, things I would ask him to tell me, if he were here . . ." I see a herd of kids rising up from their seats and making their way to the front of the church dressed in their Sunday best. The scene lands somewhere in between a Norman Rockwell painting and a Precious Moments figurine.

This is exactly what is not happening in this text. Yes, the children were converging in on Jesus, but nobody was singing. The disciples rebuked the kids, shooing them away from Jesus. This made him really angry. One of my colleagues has an acronym he uses when he is about to lose his religion: OTVOBI. It means "On the Verge of Being Infuriated." Mark uses the very harsh term "indignant" to describe Jesus' emotional state.

When Jesus saw this, he was indignant.

Earlier, Jesus took something of a pro-death penalty position for anyone who causes children to stumble (i.e., better that they have a millstone hung around their neck and be thrown into the sea, a.k.a. concrete boots). In the first century, children had no status. They would have been considered like property. Some think Jesus is conferring status on children. I don't think so. He's actually saying status is the problem. Jesus all at once protects the vulnerability of children and extols the seeming non-value of their powerlessness.

"Truly I tell you, anyone who will not receive the kingdom of God like a little child will never enter it."

purity of heart

A child brought nothing to the table to offer in any kind of exchange. A child possessed no merit that would permit them access to any mode of privilege. A child could only receive what was given them. They had no claim on anything. Jesus lifts this state of being as the requirement for entering the kingdom of God. Any merit or claim or power of any kind must be checked at the door of the entry into the kingdom of God. The most powerful people in society can only enter the kingdom of God if they can receive the invitation in the same way that the most powerless people do.

Consider this hypothetical scenario. You've worked all your life to save enough money to be able to have a comfortable and even indulgent retirement. You have everything you want and more money in the bank than you could spend in two lifetimes. You didn't win the lottery. You earned every dime of it and you are living the dream. Now suppose you came to the border of a kingdom of unparalleled prosperity, a place of abundance for all who lived there with infinite room for more. As you approach the gate you see hundreds of people crossing the border without issue, only they are mostly poor people and children and prostitutes and the sort. At the border, you are welcomed to enter the kingdom, only they want you to know one thing before crossing over. Your wealth, privilege, position, and power will have no value in the new country. Because you will have no need of it, there is no need to bring it in. One more thing, in the new country, the King's promise is that you will live in this place of free abundance forever.

I think that's why Jesus picks up a child to make his point in this very adult sermon.

The Prayer

Spirit of the living God, fall afresh on me.

The Questions

- Would you enter this kingdom?

53 Getting the "A" and Failing the Course

MARK 10:17–22 ESV | And as he was setting out on his journey, a man ran up and knelt before him and asked him, "Good Teacher, what must I do to inherit eternal life?" And Jesus said to him, "Why do you call me good? No one is good except God alone. You know the commandments: 'Do not murder, Do not commit adultery, Do not steal, Do not bear false witness, Do not defraud, Honor your father and mother.'" And he said to him, "Teacher, all these I have kept from my youth." And Jesus, looking at him, loved him, and said to him, "You lack one thing: go, sell all that you have and give to the poor, and you will have treasure in heaven; and come, follow me." Disheartened by the saying, he went away sorrowful, for he had great possessions.

Consider This

The more I read this text, the less sure I am that Jesus actually wanted this man to sell everything he had and give it to the poor.

And the more I read this text, the more sure I am that what Jesus most wanted this man to do was to follow him.

This man is living in a performance paradigm. What must I do to inherit eternal life? How can I achieve it? Obviously he thought it had to do with some measure of being good. Clearly he had done good. He had followed the rules from childhood. We know he respected authority from the way he ran up to Jesus and knelt down before him. After all, it's the good son who inherits the estate, right?

I'm going to speculate at this point. I think this man was like so many others in that keeping the Law for him had become about keeping the Law—for him. He wanted to measure up, to meet the requirements in order to achieve (or inherit) the good life. He got the "A," yet he knew deep down he was failing the course. He had everything he wanted, yet he still hadn't found what he was looking for. He was asking Jesus for the next assignment or accomplishment or test for his religious resume.

For Jesus, the Law is never about the Law. The Law is an expression of the character of the Law Giver. The character of the Law Giver is holy love; the kind of love that gives life. Now, because the Law Giver is about love, the Law actually becomes the training ground for this kind of life. What the Law wants to do is to train me to live my life with your highest good in mind and to train you to live your life with my highest good in mind. The Law is never about compliance for my sake but obedience for your sake. The Law is meant to train us to love in such a way that the Law is no longer needed because it has become written on our hearts. It's why the Golden Rule is to "do unto others as you would have them do unto you." That's why when Jesus is asked about the Greatest Law he renders it according to the love of God and neighbor.

When we make keeping the Law about keeping the Law, it's all about the self-interest of getting the "A." This is how you get the "A" and fail the course. You see the man's question tips us off to the big problem we are dealing with. "What must I do to inherit eternal life?" Did you catch it? The big problem is self-interest. This is the big problem of the human race.

This man had a ton of money. Let's just stipulate he was a billionaire of his time. I think we could be pretty sure he kept the Law on tithing—10 percent. He can check the box, yet at the same time he can live in extraordinary comfort while men, women, and children are starving to death all around him. Sure, he probably has a foundation and gives to charity and has his name on buildings and bridges and such, but deep down when everything gets quiet (which is probably rare because of the pain of it), he knows that he knows that though he has everything he ever wanted he still hasn't found the life he is looking for. This man is insecure at the core of his being and has given his life to amassing external security only to find it actually produced more internal insecurity.

Sure, he will throw the poor a bone, yet even that is to make him feel better about himself.

Jesus knows. He sees straight through the religious smoke screen. This man doesn't have wealth. Wealth has him and it is literally choking the life out of him. Jesus saw the poisoned fruit of his self-interested life and he went straight for the roots of the idolatry that had come to define his identity: his wealth.

And Jesus, looking at him, loved him, and said to him, "You lack one thing: go, sell all that you have and give to the poor, and you will have treasure in heaven; and come, follow me."

In my humble opinion—Jesus said, "Go sell everything you have and give to the poor" in the same way he said, "It is easier for a camel to go through the eye of a needle than for someone who is rich to enter the kingdom of God." Jesus is a master of overstating his case to make his point while never overplaying his hand.

It turns out the law-keeper, who was actually a law-breaker, found himself kneeling in the presence of the Law Giver who loved him enough to tell him the grace-filled truth. It's like he was saying to the man, "You will never find life until you release your death grip on the very thing that's killing you—your attachment to your wealth. The life you seek will come through following me, and for you it begins right here. Can you let go?"

Knowing that Jesus is looking upon us and loving us in these same ways, let's invite the Holy Spirit to search us out with some challenging questions.

The Prayer

Spirit of the living God, fall afresh on me.

The Questions

- On what foundation have we built our life and security and identity? What could we never imagine letting go of?
- What do we possess that really possesses us? What do we most fear the Lord might ask us to release? Why do we fear it?

54 | How Jesus Kicks Our Value System to the Curb

MARK 10:23–31 NRSV | Then Jesus looked around and said to his disciples, "How hard it will be for those who have wealth to enter the kingdom of God!" And the disciples were perplexed at these words. But Jesus said to them again, "Children, how hard it is to enter the kingdom of God! It is easier for a camel to go through the eye of a needle than for someone who is rich to enter the kingdom of God." They were greatly astounded and said to one another, "Then who can be saved?" Jesus looked at them and said, "For mortals it is impossible, but not for God; for God all things are possible."

Peter began to say to him, "Look, we have left everything and followed you." Jesus said, "Truly I tell you, there is no one who has left house or brothers or sisters or mother or father or children or fields, for my sake and for the sake of the good news, who will not receive a hundredfold now in this age— houses, brothers and sisters, mothers and children, and fields, with persecutions—and in the age to come eternal life. But many who are first will be last, and the last will be first."

Consider This

We left off in Mark with the man of great wealth coming before Jesus with his query about inheriting eternal life. Bottom line: Jesus was willing to let the wealthy man go away sad.

With these few sentences Jesus crushes the conventional wisdom of the day. In those days (as in our own), people tended to equate wealth as a sign of God's favor and as the fruit of a righteous life. The corollary also rang true: poverty was a sign of the absence of God's favor and the bitter fruit of sin.

We need to remember at this point how Jesus had systematically taken on this value system. He went to the poor and the lepers and the sick and unleashed extravagant blessing on them. In today's text, he takes the system on from the angle of the rich. This comment about the impossibility of rich people entering the kingdom of God would have been nothing less than stupefying to those gathered. Jaws would have hit the floor everywhere. Jesus said the exact opposite of all they had been taught.

The Twelve looked at one another with sheer incredulity.

They were greatly astounded and said to one another, "Then who can be saved?"

Wealth was not the sign of blessing, rather it was the source of burden. This was truly an aha moment.

The kingdom of God cannot be understood as an extension of the kingdom of the world with a little Jesus overlay. The kingdom of God cannot be understood as a projection of even the best and most fair minded merit system we can imagine. Bottom line: No one has any claim on the kingdom of God. In fact, it's impossible for anyone to enter the kingdom of God on their own terms.

Jesus looked at them and said, "For mortals it is impossible, but not for God; for God all things are possible."

The kingdom of God belongs exclusively to those who will unconditionally and absolutely belong to the God of the kingdom. In the end, this is not about divesting oneself of wealth, but entrusting oneself to God. Wealth, like nothing else, can get in the way of this, which is precisely why our wealth must be entrusted to God—whatever that means and whatever it takes.

Peter began to say to him, "Look, we have left everything and followed you."

At first glance it feels like Peter was contending for some kind of claim here; something akin to "you owe us." In response, Jesus doesn't so much rebuke as he reassures. All the possibilities of God reside with those who place all of their possibilities in his hands. On second thought, I think Peter was saying just that—we have trusted you with everything, Jesus.

Jesus reassures them by saying in effect, "And everything I have, little flock, I am giving to you."

This is extravagant exchange. The celebrated missionary turned martyr Jim Elliot said it best when he said, "He is no fool who gives what he cannot keep to gain what he cannot lose."

The Prayer

Spirit of the living God, fall afresh on me.

The Questions

- Jesus says it is hard to enter the kingdom of God. Why do we tend to speak and act like it is so easy?

How Jesus Wants Us to Respond to Hard Things

55

MARK 10:32–45 | They were on their way up to Jerusalem, with Jesus leading the way, and the disciples were astonished, while those who followed were afraid. Again he took the Twelve aside and told them what was going to happen to him. "We are going up to Jerusalem," he said, "and the Son of Man will be delivered over to the chief priests and the teachers of the law. They will condemn him to death and will hand him over to the Gentiles, who will mock him and spit on him, flog him and kill him. Three days later he will rise."

Then James and John, the sons of Zebedee, came to him. "Teacher," they said, "we want you to do for us whatever we ask."

"What do you want me to do for you?" he asked.

They replied, "Let one of us sit at your right and the other at your left in your glory."

"You don't know what you are asking," Jesus said. "Can you drink the cup I drink or be baptized with the baptism I am baptized with?"

"We can," they answered.

Jesus said to them, "You will drink the cup I drink and be baptized with the baptism I am baptized with, but to sit at my right or left is not for me to grant. These places belong to those for whom they have been prepared."

When the ten heard about this, they became indignant with James and John. Jesus called them together and said, "You know that those who are regarded as rulers of the Gentiles lord it over them, and their high officials exercise authority over them. Not so with you. Instead, whoever wants to become great among you must be your servant, and whoever wants to be first must be slave of all. For even the Son of Man did not come to be served, but to serve, and to give his life as a ransom for many."

Consider This

I think he was hoping maybe the third time would be the charm. This was the third time Jesus pulled his twelve disciples aside and gave them the explicit inside track on what was about to happen.

You remember the last time he told them this—they were afraid to ask him about it. Then there was the time before that, after Peter made his famous confession of Jesus as the Messiah.

> He then began to teach them that the Son of Man must suffer many things and be rejected by the elders, the chief priests and the teachers of the law, and that he must be killed and after three days rise again. He spoke plainly about this, and Peter took him aside and began to rebuke him. (Mark 8:31–32)

Today a similarly absurd response on the part of the disciples. Jesus all but spells out Golgotha and all they can think about is glory.

It all makes me wonder what kind of response Jesus hoped to get from his disciples in response to this disclosure. Let's ponder some possible responses.

They might have responded to him with more questions like, "What is the meaning of this?" or, "Why are you telling us this?" or, "What do you want us to do?" or, "What must we do to prepare for this?" or, "Why does this have to happen?"

They might have offered various solutions like, "How about we go back to Galilee and get back to work?" or, "Surely we can make some kind of deal with the Sanhedrin to avoid this" or, "Let's put our heads together and try to solve this problem."

Then there are the more empathic approaches, like maybe they could have fallen on their faces and cried with him over this devastating news, or maybe they could have embraced him and expressed their sadness and sorrow, or asked how he was doing with this prognosis and so on.

And, of course, there are the optimistic and opportunistic approaches like, "You can do it, Jesus! It will only hurt for a little while and it will all be worth it in the end!" or, *"Let one of us sit at your right and the other at your left in your glory."*

My hunch on what he was looking for? I think he wanted them to take him by the hand, look him in the eye, and from the depth of their hearts say something like, "Jesus, we are with you every step of the way, come what may, no matter what, to the very end. The cross before us, the world behind us, no turning back. Let's do this!"

The truth is that there is a cross in all of our paths almost all of the time and if it's not in our path at the moment, it's in someone else's path we can help share. There are hard promises we must keep, difficult roads we must traverse, and painful decisions we must make against our self-interest, all in the interest of loving God and loving others. They are different from and yet in keeping with the decision Jesus made to go to Jerusalem and endure the cross on the way to resurrection. Along the way, the hard ways will be made easier, the heavy loads will become lighter, and the easy ways out will become more and more absurd to us.

And the best part of all is that he says to us exactly what he would have us say to him, "Friend, I am with you every step of the way, come what may, no matter what, to the very end. The cross before us, the world behind us, no turning back. Let's do this!"

The Prayer
Spirit of the living God, fall afresh on me.

The Questions
- The way of the cross is the hard way, right? Why do we want it to be easy?

Why Blindness Is the Real Problem

56

MARK 10:46–52 ESV | And they came to Jericho. And as he was leaving Jericho with his disciples and a great crowd, Bartimaeus, a blind beggar, the son of Timaeus, was sitting by the roadside. And when he heard that it was Jesus of Nazareth, he began to cry out and say, "Jesus, Son of David, have mercy on me!" And many rebuked him, telling him to be silent. But he cried out all the more, "Son of David, have mercy on me!" And Jesus stopped and said, "Call him." And they called the blind man, saying to him, "Take heart. Get up; he is calling you." And throwing off his cloak, he sprang up and came to Jesus. And Jesus said to him, "What do you want me to do for you?" And the blind man said to him, "Rabbi, let me recover my sight." And Jesus said to him, "Go your way; your faith has made you well." And immediately he recovered his sight and followed him on the way.

Consider This

Not only was he poor, but he was blind, which landed Bartimaeus in the ill-fated category of the poorest of the poor. Helpless and hopeless, he had become something of a piece of discarded furniture on the side of the road people didn't even notice anymore. He was just another beggar. You know what I'm talking about—the guy at the busy intersection holding the "Will Work for Food" sign who really just wants your spare change.

And here's the first big problem. It's not his blindness, but ours that gets in the way of the working of the Holy Spirit. No one in the crowd that day had anything remotely close to "eyes to see" and "ears to hear." As Bartimaeus cried out, the people told him to shut up. Not only did they not want to see him, they didn't want to hear him either.

Whether Jesus saw him or heard him first we know not, nor does it matter. He wants us to see and hear Bartimaeus now. He wants us to understand the ways the Holy Spirit searches to and fro for the blind Bartimaeus types. What do I mean by that? Bartimaeus was not looking for the next handout. He wanted liberation from his situation. Maybe he was tired of victimhood. Maybe he had come to the place where he was sick of living alms gift to alms. He knew he could not solve his own problem, yet he also knew he had to cry out for something more than help for his symptoms. He knew he needed a fundamental change.

And Jesus said to him, "What do you want me to do for you?" And the blind man said to him, "Rabbi, let me recover my sight."

It's got me thinking . . . what if I asked this question to the next beggar I encountered, "What do you want me to do for you?" And what if he said, "I need $10." That strikes me as an invitation to perpetuate his problem. It's the easiest thing for him to ask for and, frankly, the easiest thing I could give him. But I think it's probably not the kind of thing Jesus is going for.

Now, what if he said, "I need to get something to eat." In my opinion, this isn't the kind of faith Jesus is looking for either. Still, I could go get him some food and it would be a faithful act of service.

But what if he said, "I need help getting a job." This is where it gets harder. This is the kind of faith Jesus looks for among those in need—people who are looking for real change, who have thought through what they most need and because they know they are stuck without help, they are bold enough to ask for it. Do you see what happens now? His faith hit the ball into my court and now it becomes about my faith.

For a disciple of Jesus Christ, this is where the proverbial road meets the rubber. Honestly, it's so much easier for me to wait for the light to turn green and move on and just tell myself the story about this guy that I have always told myself—that he's where he is as a consequence of his choices and it's not my problem and the price of helping him is just too high and, besides, I give my money to the church who is supposed to help solve these situations.

"Go your way; your faith has made you well."

I want us to note that faith is not some kind of magic or some sort of internal substance that we either have enough of or not in order for God to work. Faith heals precisely because it requires something more of us than asking for a temporary fix to a systemic problem. Faith brings people to a place beyond the symptoms to the source of a problem. It requires of them the act of moving toward a possibility that was hitherto unseeable to them. It changes things in a permanent way. Despite Bartimaeus's physical blindness (or maybe because of it), his faith enabled him to see something even physical sight could not see—the possibilities of the mercy of God.

And immediately he recovered his sight and followed him on the way.

See what happened? Bartimaeus went from sitting beside the road to following Jesus along the road. That's the big deal.

A final note: faith also heals the healer. Nothing makes a person more well than helping another person to get well in the name of Jesus. We must get beyond the thin solutions that only serve to make us feel better that we did something. Those kinds of solutions only further serve the problem. We must press into the deeper need of the other. This is not easy. It gets messy. This is the big deal. It means taking on the mind and mentality of Jesus who teaches us that we come "not to be served but to serve."

I think the real problem is not the blindness of Bartimaeus but our own blindness. Maybe the best thing we can do today would be to say to Jesus, "Lord, I want to see."

The Prayer
Spirit of the living God, fall afresh on me.

The Questions
- How does this challenge your discipleship? Where is your faith rising up to meet the rising faith of someone else in need today?
- What holds you back?

Living in Light of the Larger Story

57

MARK 11:1–10 NRSV | When they were approaching Jerusalem, at Bethphage and Bethany, near the Mount of Olives, he sent two of his disciples and said to them, "Go into the village ahead of you, and immediately as you enter it, you will find tied there a colt that has never been ridden; untie it and bring it. If anyone says to you, 'Why are you doing this?' just say this, 'The Lord needs it and will send it back here immediately.'" They went away and found a colt tied near a door, outside in the street. As they were untying it, some of the bystanders said to them, "What are you doing, untying the colt?" They told them what Jesus had said; and they allowed them to take it. Then they brought the colt to Jesus and threw their cloaks on it; and he sat on it. Many people spread their cloaks on the road, and others spread leafy branches that they had cut in the fields. Then those who went ahead and those who followed were shouting,

> "Hosanna!
> Blessed is the one who comes in the name of the Lord!
> Blessed is the coming kingdom of our ancestor David!
> Hosanna in the highest heaven!"

Consider This

It is really challenging (if not impossible) to read the Gospel from the beginning, going through it for the first time as an unknowing pilgrim reader. We know how the story ends and, because of that, we tend to interpret the story from the vantage point of knowing the ending. We call it a "triumphal entry" only because we know the resurrection is on the other side. But imagine heading into it all without knowing.

It's interesting how our lives are lived in just the opposite fashion. We don't know how it will all turn out and so we can only interpret the future from the perspective of the past, and because to one degree or another, we have a broken past we tend to see the future through broken lenses.

Of course, this is where our faith comes into play. Faith means we do know how it will all end up, because we know the bigger story in which the smaller stories of our lives are

Do I have

being played out. Faith means living in the here and now in the distinctive kinds of ways (i.e., Christian) one would live if they knew ahead of time how the story would end. In the case of the Christian story, that's why we have the possibility of such freedom, joy, and peace. In fact, if we don't presently enjoy some level of freedom, joy, and peace in the present, we might want to ask ourselves some deeper questions about whether we really do have faith in the way it will all turn out (or if our freedom, joy, and peace is just the best version that money can buy).

However, when we are living in the here and now in the distinctive kinds of ways (i.e., Christian) we would live if we knew ahead of time how the story would end, the people around us will often not understand. Why? Because we will be living in ways that are counterintuitive to the ways of the world. It's why Jesus disciples his disciples in these distinctive kinds of ways—like the last will be first, and the one who serves will be the greatest, and whoever loses their self for my sake will find it. This is not some bloated idealism. This is the way of faith. This is the way human beings were intended to live. And Jesus shows us the possibility of all of it. As I have said many times, "As Jesus was on earth, so we are becoming," and, "Come, Holy Spirit!"

So what does all of this have to do with today's text? Nothing and everything. As Jesus sat atop that donkey and rode into Jerusalem, no one around him had any idea of what he was really doing. They thought they did. They had some kind of outcome in mind, but they were wrong. They had a good sense of how the big story would end, but they completely misunderstood how it would ultimately get there. In fact, the complete opposite happened. Their leader was executed as a common criminal.

Only Jesus knew what lay ahead in Jerusalem and beyond and he knew how it would all end, yet he still had to live it out by faith. This is why later in Scripture he is called the author and pioneer of our faith (see Hebrews 12:2). He is the One who walked the way, living in the here and now in the distinctive kinds of ways one would live if they knew ahead of time how the story would end. That's why we follow him. That's why we keep our eyes fixed on him. It's why we can agree with Paul that "our light and momentary troubles are achieving for us an eternal glory that far outweighs them all" (2 Cor. 4:17).

The miracle of the life hid with God in Christ is that in the midst of the greatest hardships and pain the divine promise empowers in us the ability to live in freedom, joy, and peace, despite it all.

The Prayer

Spirit of the living God, fall afresh on me.

The Questions

- What kind of outlook do you have on the future? Is it filled with hope despite what you presently see? Or is your outlook fueled by mere optimism and positive thinking?
- Do you see the glorious end despite the inglorious middle you may presently face?

On Splitting Hell Wide Open with a Baptismal Certificate in Your Hands

58

MARK 11:11–17 | Jesus entered Jerusalem and went into the temple courts. He looked around at everything, but since it was already late, he went out to Bethany with the Twelve.

unproductive Christians

The next day as they were leaving Bethany, Jesus was hungry. Seeing in the distance a fig tree in leaf, he went to find out if it had any fruit. When he reached it, he found nothing but leaves, because it was not the season for figs. Then he said to the tree, "May no one ever eat fruit from you again." And his disciples heard him say it.

On reaching Jerusalem, Jesus entered the temple courts and began driving out those who were buying and selling there. He overturned the tables of the money changers and the benches of those selling doves, and would not allow anyone to carry merchandise through the temple courts. And as he taught them, he said, "Is it not written: 'My house will be called a house of prayer for all nations'? But you have made it 'a den of robbers.'"

Consider This

Two things we must ever guard against as the followers of Jesus: soft-pedaling or hard-lining the hard teachings of

Jesus. We do a disservice to the church and damage to the gospel when we err on either side.

We must recognize that Jesus said many things that require keen interpretation and nuanced understanding. We must do our best to understand the things he said in their original first-century context and in the way they would have been understood by the ears who actually heard the words come out of his mouth.

Jesus cursing a fig tree that was not bearing fruit out of fruit-bearing season is a tough teaching. It's one of those texts we neither want to under interpret or overplay or, even worse, sweep under the rug.

My first remembrance of this text came in my glory days as a youth pastor. One Sunday night I decided to take my youth to a youth revival down the street at the Baptist church. The guest revivalist preacher curiously chose this story about the fig tree for his revival text. He set up a stirring contrast between fruit and leaves, equating leaves without fruit as talking the talk without walking the walk. Leaves without fruit is the form of religion without the power; going through the motions of church without living in the way of Jesus. "Leaves," he said over and over again, "will never get it done."

About midway through, the preacher, drenched in sweat, looked out at the congregation of half-asleep teenagers, upped the decibel level of his voice a couple of clicks, and proceeded to dress them down. "What Jesus said to Israel, he today says to you: You are a people flourishing with leaves yet failing to bear fruit." "In fact," and he raised his voice another four decibels, "there are a lot of you sitting here in these pews tonight . . ." He paused, as if entering a kind of internal debate as to whether he would say what he was thinking. Then he said it, "Okay, I'm just going to call it. There are a lot of you sitting here in these pews tonight . . . you are going to split hell wide open with a baptismal certificate in your hand."

You could have heard a pin drop. I must confess, at the time I was more than a little bit mortified. All of my stereotypes about Baptist youth revivalists had come true to the tenth power. Then he gave the invitation, further elucidating his perilous prophetic warning about having all the appearances of being a Christian with none of the authentic proof. I watched in a kind of Holy Spirit stupor as one by one the kids I brought to the revival made their way to the altar to, in all likelihood, give their lives to Jesus for the very first time, with their baptismal certificates—in a manner of speaking—in their hands.

Twenty-five years later, I look back at that moment as a turning point for me. What at the time seemed like a gross overstatement of Jesus' case, I today look at as a pretty fair rendering of what he meant.

On the evening after his arrival in Jerusalem, Jesus paid a quiet visit to the grand edifice of the temple. He knew it had gone off the rails and I suspect he dreaded to some degree what had to be done. I suspect he didn't sleep much that night. I suspect he woke wrestling with his Father about what had to happen and how it needed to be done. Jesus knew he would be signing his own death warrant if he went through with it. And, on his way to the temple, he ran into this fig tree.

Here's what I think happened as he reached through the leafy foliage to fruitlessly search for a fig. I think the Holy Spirit flashed images of prophets and their fig tree pronouncements through his mind like Jeremiah and Hosea and Joel and Micah and Isaiah.

It was as though the Holy Spirit was saying, "Here's your sign."

Then he said to the tree, "May no one ever eat fruit from you again." And his disciples heard him say it.

Despite all the gracious warnings they had been given, Israel had not borne fruit, nor would they ever in season or out. They would split hell wide open with their baptismal certificates in their hands, declaring Abraham as their father with their lips while desecrating his faith with their lives.

John Wesley made it a practice for the early Methodists to ask one another hard questions. At the top of his list was this one: Am I consciously or unconsciously creating the impression that I am better than others? In other words, am I a hypocrite? Translation: Am I really the person I'm projecting on my Instagram?

The Prayer

Spirit of the living God, fall afresh on me.

The Questions

- Is your life all about leaves, or are you bearing fruit?

- Are you more concerned with how you are coming off on the outside than with who you are becoming on the inside?

The Difference between the Power of Prayer and the Power of God

59

MARK 11:18–25 ESV | And the chief priests and the scribes heard it and were seeking a way to destroy him, for they feared him, because all the crowd was astonished at his teaching. And when evening came they went out of the city.

As they passed by in the morning, they saw the fig tree withered away to its roots. And Peter remembered and said to him, "Rabbi, look! The fig tree that you cursed has withered." And Jesus answered them, "Have faith in God. Truly, I say to you, whoever says to this mountain, 'Be taken up and thrown into the sea,' and does not doubt in his heart, but believes that what he says will come to pass, it will be done for him. Therefore I tell you, whatever you ask in prayer, believe that you have received it, and it will be yours. And whenever you stand praying, forgive, if you have anything against anyone, so that your Father also who is in heaven may forgive you your trespasses."

Consider This

How are we to understand this?

"Truly, I say to you, whoever says to this mountain, 'Be taken up and thrown into the sea,' and does not doubt in his heart, but believes that what he says will come to pass, it will be done for him. Therefore I tell you, whatever you ask in prayer, believe that you have received it, and it will be yours."

If ever there were a proof text for the name-it-and-claim-it crowd, this is it. In fact, entire theological systems and faith movements have been built by a few verses like these and others strung together. However, I think any biblical interpreter worth his or her salt would quickly say, "Not so fast!" My dear friend Dr. Ben Witherington III often puts it this way, "A text taken out of context becomes a pretext for anything you want it to say."

So what's going on here? Remember, we are coming to the end of the three-year period of discipleship for the Twelve. They have been schooled in the nature of the sovereignty of God. They have been taught and trained in the ways of the kingdom of God. And let's remember the bigger context at work. In the last entry, Jesus cursed the fig tree and cleaned house at the temple. In contrast to the religious machinations of the temple in which Israel placed so much confidence, Jesus tells his disciples to, *"Have faith in God."*

As they stood there on the Mount of Olives looking at the withered fig tree that would indeed never bear fruit again, they couldn't but help to have seen the towering temple across the valley in the mighty Jerusalem. Jesus, in essence, told his disciples the whole project had become a house of cards that would soon come crashing down. Don't have faith in the corrupted system. *"Have faith in God."*

This is the big deal—the whole point of discipleship. As they followed Jesus, he showed them what God was like every step of the way. Discipleship is learning by Word and Spirit who God is and what God is like. It is learning to trust the true God. This is manifest through a life of prayer, which is the hidden way the life of faith works. The way of faith depends on the life of prayer as one's heartbeat depends on one's breath. Dr. William Lane, one of my teachers through this Gospel of Mark, said it well: "When prayer is the source of faith's power and the means of its strength, God's sovereignty is its only restriction."

"Therefore I tell you, whatever you ask in prayer, believe that you have received it, and it will be yours."

When a follower of Jesus lives immersed in the Word of God and is animated by the Spirit of God, their prayers—with ever-increasing resonance—ring true to the will of God. God funds his will through the faith-filled prayers of his people. We must learn to think of prayer not in the terms of the power of our faith but the framework of the faithfulness of our God. Prayer is that constant abiding conversation Jesus wants to have with us all the time. It is simpler than we could ever have imagined, yet more consuming than we can conceive. With today's text, Jesus teaches us what it means to be people who live and love with power. There is one other restriction, though.

"And whenever you stand praying, forgive, if you have anything against anyone, so that your Father also who is in heaven may forgive you your trespasses."

The only blockade to the way of faith inspired by the life of prayer is unforgiveness. To the degree we withhold forgiveness from others, we deny it to ourselves. As has been aptly said, "Unforgiveness is drinking poison and expecting it to kill the other person." A final practical note on forgiveness. Forgiveness is not saying what happened was okay. It doesn't mean everything is hunky-dory after. It's not about kissing and making up. Forgiveness is the willful decision to cease retaliating in any form against the person who harmed you. (That includes harboring bitterness and anger fantasies, etc.)

Is prayer more about something you say (which is not a bad thing), or is it taking the shape of constant conversation?

Invite the Holy Spirit to search your spirit and ferret out any unforgiveness festering there. Are you ready to let that go? Can you confess unforgiveness as a sin and invite the Holy Spirit to cleanse you of its poison and to empower you to let go of your need to pay them back if only in your mind? It's just not worth it to hold on to unforgiveness. Don't waste another minute of your life.

The Prayer

Spirit of the living God, fall afresh on me.

The Questions

- At what point in your life right now do you most need to have faith in God?
- What practical steps does this mean you need to consider taking now?

On the Power of Telling an Alternative Story

MARK 11:27–33 NRSV | Again they came to Jerusalem. As he was walking in the temple, the chief priests, the scribes, and the elders came to him and said, "By what authority are you doing these things? Who gave you this authority to do them?" Jesus said to them, "I will ask you one question; answer me, and I will tell you by what authority I do these things. Did the baptism of John come from heaven, or was it of human origin? Answer me." They argued with one another, "If we say, 'From heaven,' he will say, 'Why then did you not believe him?' But shall we say, 'Of human origin'?"—they were afraid of the crowd, for all regarded John as truly a prophet. So they answered Jesus, "We do not know." And Jesus said to them, "Neither will I tell you by what authority I am doing these things."

Consider This

Ivan Illich was a twentieth-century Roman Catholic priest and philosopher from Austria. He was once asked what is the most revolutionary way to change society. Is it violent revolution or is it gradual reform? He gave a careful answer. "Neither . . . If you want to change a society, then you must tell an alternative story."

Today's text strikes this chord in a most dissonant fashion. Today we see the classic confrontation of the ages: the authorities who have power over the people versus the ones whose authority is recognized by the people. It usually sets up as the reformers versus the revolutionaries.

It's easy to vilify the Sanhedrin, but unfair. Try to see it through their lens. They clearly have an agenda for reform. Their reverence for the Word of God was second to none. They wanted to spread scriptural holiness across the land. They lived for the glory of God to be spread across the earth and all of their reforms were to this end.

All of this evokes images of the 2016 election cycle in America and the Republican debates. On the stage we saw nine reformers and one would-be revolutionary. It is why some people love Donald Trump. They are sick to death of the system and they don't really believe it can be reformed. They want a kind of revolution and Trump represents that to them. The leadership of the Republican party plays something of the role of the Sanhedrin here. They want to know where Trump gets his legitimate authority. Of course, Trump's ugly threat is to take his revolution to an Independent party and go to it from there. This could be pushed with all sorts of interesting implications and insights. However, we will not find any government with the capacity to tell the alternative story we are looking for short of the now-and-yet-coming kingdom of God. Didn't Isaiah say something like, "and the government will be upon his shoulders"?

John the Baptist was something of a reformer-revolutionary, yet he knew he was not the one to lead the revolution. He prophesied of the Coming One. The baptism the Messiah would bring would be of a different order than John's water baptism. It would bear the character of fire. As a consequence, Jesus could not help but be understood by the people as the leader of a revolution who would restore the kingdom to Israel. John's dismayed message to Jesus from prison, "Are you the one? Or should we expect another?" signifies this situation. Right up to the very end the people expected to see Jesus take back the nation from Rome and institute the kingdom of God on earth. This evoked great fear in the hearts of the reformers (i.e., the Sanhedrin). Not only would this independent movement erode their power base, it would likely lead to the end of the nation.

Here's what no one saw coming, despite Jesus' explicit and clear indications. Jesus was not bringing a reform of the present system, nor was he bringing a revolutionary overthrow of the religious establishment and the Roman interlopers. Jesus told an alternative story. Jesus, through his words, deeds, life, and coming death was telling the story not of reform or revolution, but resurrection.

I acknowledge this is a bit of a ponderous thinker entry, but it bears immense practical significance for the ways we live out our lives in the midst of the crumbling institutions all around us—from marriage to schools to the workplace to the government and the economy. Reform is good but will never get the job done. Revolution is tempting but never ultimately works, for it merely replaces one power stronghold with another equally corrupt one.

In the face of these options we are called to be persons and collectively a people of the cross—which is to say persons and a people who live out the powerful way of death and resurrection in the everyday world—people who have died to the agenda of sin and death and who are gloriously alive to the agenda of resurrection and life. To the present generations of the people of God, this is our shift, our time, and our passing opportunity to tell the alternative story of the cross in the most compelling and beautiful and demonstrably powerful way possible. Amen? Amen!

The Prayer

Spirit of the living God, fall afresh on me.

The Questions

* Isn't this what discipleship in the way of Jesus is all about? Death to the kingdom of sin and death and self, and resurrection into the powerful kingdom of the holy love of God?
* What does this look like in application?

Vineyard - Nation of Israel
God - The owner who planted
Tenants - Israel's Religious leaders
Servants - Ramined faithful
The other - Gentiles   The Son - Jesus

Why You Really Don't Own Anything

61

MARK 12:1–12 | Jesus then began to speak to them in parables: "A man planted a vineyard. He put a wall around it, dug a pit for the winepress and built a watchtower. Then he rented the vineyard to some farmers and moved to another place. At harvest time he sent a servant to the tenants to collect from them some of the fruit of the vineyard. But they seized him, beat him and sent him away empty-handed. Then he sent another servant to them; they struck this man on the head and treated him shamefully. He sent still another, and that one they killed. He sent many others; some of them they beat, others they killed.

"He had one left to send, a son, whom he loved. He sent him last of all, saying, 'They will respect my son.'

"But the tenants said to one another, 'This is the heir. Come, let's kill him, and the inheritance will be ours.' So they took him and killed him, and threw him out of the vineyard.

"What then will the owner of the vineyard do? He will come and kill those tenants and give the vineyard to others. Haven't you read this passage of Scripture:

"'The stone the builders rejected
  has become the cornerstone;
the Lord has done this,
  and it is marvelous in our eyes'?"

Then the chief priests, the teachers of the law and the elders looked for a way to arrest him because they knew he had spoken the parable against them. But they were afraid of the crowd; so they left him and went away.

Consider This

When you are a landowner and you rent your land to be farmed by tenant farmers, you enter into a very ancient, quite common, yet highly nuanced relationship. I understand this because I come from a long line of farmers. Our family has been on both sides of the equation—as the tenant farmers on some occasions and as the landowners on others. Allow me to raise a few of the fundamental yet sophisticated assumptions: (1) the landowner expects the tenant farmer to farm the land as though it were his/her own; and (2) the landowner expects the tenant farmer to remember this land is not his own but that he must maintain the highest standards of accountability to the landowner.

Permit me a sidebar comment that potentially cracks the nut of the whole parable. This is the way God expects us to think of our own lives and everything we have. I am not my own. I belong to God. God entrusts me with all that I am and all that I have. I own nothing yet I am responsible to steward it all with the same fidelity and fruitfulness as though I owned it all. God expects a fruitful return from our lives—for our gain, the good of our neighbors, and to the end bringing God glory. This is the life of discipleship and the way of the cross. Life can be profoundly simple and unimaginably good if we are willing to trust God, die to ourselves and our self-interests, and be raised to the life of Jesus Christ by the power of the Holy Spirit. It can be insanely complicated and unutterably conflicted if we drift from the fundamental assumptions of this relationship, forgetting who is who and whose is what.

In truth, we will flourish as the followers of Jesus and thrive in the kind of life we were made for to the extent we live into this reality. To the extent we do not live from these core assumptions on which everything else is built, we will become arrested in our development and fail to become the people God imagined when he made us. We will come to the end of our days only to realize we have wasted our lives. The beautiful thing? It's never too late to get this right. The even more beautiful thing about getting it right? God will work retroactively to take the broken ways we have lived and bring blessing from them for others' sake.

When Jesus told the Jewish leaders this story, they knew exactly where he was going with it, and it infuriated them. Why? They knew the deplorable track record of their leaders through history. They thought they were different; that they could somehow get it right in God's name without doing it according to God's will and ways. Despite all of their highly visible devotion to God, their lives were devoid of his presence. Despite the ornate beauty and grandeur of the temple, in a manner of speaking, God had left the building a long time ago.

In point of fact, in their minds, the landowner was dead.

"But the tenants said to one another, 'This is the heir. Come, let's kill him, and the inheritance will be ours.' So they took him and killed him, and threw him out of the vineyard."

Anyone knows if the landowner was still alive, killing his heir would not mean anything. It would still belong to the landowner. Clearly, they thought the landowner was dead. In consequence of their assumption, if they could kill the heir, the land would be theirs. It's something akin to the legal doctrine known as squatter's rights.

All of this brings us back to the three strategies noted previously: reform, revolution, and resurrection. The reforms of the religious leaders actually turned out to be their own revolt or revolution against God. Jesus introduced the new strategy which had been there all along: death and resurrection.

"'The stone the builders rejected has become the cornerstone; the Lord has done this, and it is marvelous in our eyes'?"

Are you living the profoundly simple, unimaginably good life of a tenant farmer in God's kingdom or are you stuck in the insanely complicated, unutterably conflicted life of a would-be owner? Think about this with respect to the stewardship of your physical body. Think about it with respect to money. While money is not the whole tamale, it is a very effective barometer. Does your giving amount to a weak tip (a.k.a. 10 percent) while managing your reserves as though that were your part? And to be clear—raising that to a decent tip (a.k.a. 20 percent) is not the answer.

This is about coming to the place in your deepest heart and mind where you truly understand and live as though you owned nothing and stewarded everything—for the good of others and the glory of God. I think this is why Jesus said it is very hard for a rich person to enter the kingdom of God. This is what he means. It's not about selling everything you have and giving the money to the poor (unless it needs to be). This is all about abandoning ourselves to the One who loves us the most. It sounds impossible at first and, in fact, it is only possible with God.

The Prayer

Spirit of the living God, fall afresh on me.

The Questions

- What will it take to come to the understanding that you are not the owner of what you have, but the steward?

Why God and Politics Can't Be Separated

MARK 12:13–17 ESV | And they sent to him some of the Pharisees and some of the Herodians, to trap him in his talk. And they came and said to him, "Teacher, we know that you are true and do not care about anyone's opinion. For you are not swayed by appearances, but truly teach the way of God. Is it lawful to pay taxes to Caesar, or not? Should we pay them, or should we not?" But, knowing their hypocrisy, he said to

them, "Why put me to the test? Bring me a denarius and let me look at it." And they brought one. And he said to them, "Whose likeness and inscription is this?" They said to him, "Caesar's." Jesus said to them, "Render to Caesar the things that are Caesar's, and to God the things that are God's." And they marveled at him.

Consider This

From the first century to the twenty-first century, the saying holds true: the only two certainties in life are death and taxes. Jesus' detractors brought these two verities together in this confrontational question.

This tax evoked great resentment among the Jews. It was a constant reminder of their subjection to Rome. If Jesus says it's right to pay the tax, he comes off as a sell-out to Rome, which would have diminished the authority of his word in the eyes of the Sanhedrin. Had he said it's wrong to pay the tax, he would have drawn the fierce ire of Rome for an act of rebellion. The question was political in nature, but it was also theological.

But, knowing their hypocrisy, he said to them, "Why put me to the test? Bring me a denarius and let me look at it." And they brought one. And he said to them, "Whose likeness and inscription is this?" They said to him, "Caesar's."

The kicker comes with the inscription: "Tiberius Caesar Augustus, Son of the Divine Augustus" and, on the other, "Pontifex Maximus." Translation: Caesar was divine. The big question was whether paying the tax constituted an act of worship to Caesar, a recognition of his divinity. This is where the Pharisees wanted to trap him. If he said pay the tax, he implied bowing to Caesar. Jesus response was pure brilliance.

"Render to Caesar the things that are Caesar's, and to God the things that are God's."

The denarius, which bore Caesar's image, did indeed belong to Caesar. The denarius was the coin of the realm. Jesus acknowledged that to live under the governance of a state brought certain responsibilities with it, paying taxes being one of them. It's part of the cost of living. Jesus drew a major line in the sand with the rest of his statement. Give to God what is God's meant that paying a tax to Caesar with a coin bearing Caesar's image did not imply agreement with the coin's inscription that Caesar was God. The God of Israel was to Caesar as Jesus was to Caiphas.

Living under the governance of a sovereign state and observing its appropriate authority in no way constituted worship of the state's sovereign ruler. This was reserved for God alone. Caesar gets the tax. The coins belong to Caesar. The worship belongs to God. Caesar's claim to divinity is another way of trying to bar God from the politics of the state. It can't be done and, to the extent a people attempt it, they issue a death warrant for the state.

It's a long step from the first century to the twenty-first century. While our form of government isn't analogous to Caesar's, the words of Jesus hold true. Paying taxes is the cost of living in a civilized state. Patriotism can be an expression of healthy loyalty and support for national sovereignty. But we must be clear. Only the true and living God and Father of our Lord Jesus Christ is worthy of our worship. The minute the state infringes on the freedom of its people to worship God, it makes the people of God an enemy of the state. It's another conversation, but this gets us close to the context for Jesus command to "Love your enemies and pray for those who persecute you" (Matt. 5:44).

It's one thing to separate church and state, but quite another to separate faith from politics. In fact, it's the separation of church and state that enables the healthy and much-needed exercise of faith in the mix of politics and governance. Jerusalem fell because it put its religious establishment in the place of its God. Rome fell because it put its corrupted leaders in the place of the true God. America . . .

The Prayer

Spirit of the living God, fall afresh on me.

The Questions

- Where is my primary allegiance: to God or to country? Am I an American Christian (or Nigerian, Saudi Arabian, etc.) or am I a Christian American? Are my values shaped more by my country than by my faith?

Take the Long View

MARK 12:18–27 NRSV | Some Sadducees, who say there is no resurrection, came to him and asked him a question, saying, "Teacher, Moses wrote for us that if a man's brother dies, leaving a wife but no child, the man shall marry the widow and raise up children for his brother. There were seven brothers; the first married and, when he died, left no children; and the second married the widow and died, leaving no children; and the third likewise; none of the seven left children. Last of all the woman herself died. In the resurrection whose wife will she be? For the seven had married her."

Jesus said to them, "Is not this the reason you are wrong, that you know neither the scriptures nor the power of God? For when they rise from the dead, they neither marry nor are given in marriage, but are like angels in heaven. And as for the dead being raised, have you not read in the book of Moses, in the story about the bush, how God said to him, 'I am the God of Abraham, the God of Isaac, and the God of Jacob'? He is God not of the dead, but of the living; you are quite wrong."

Consider This

This is starting to feel like an episode of the popular game show *Jeopardy*. Today's question from the Sadducees brings even more drama to the plot of coconspirators surrounding Jesus.

First for a little background, the Sadducees enjoyed an aris-tocratic reputation. They strike me as the sophisticates of the

Jewish pantheon of religious players. Like the Pharisees and the Scribes, they highly valued the Scriptures though they advocated for their own interpretation.

In particular, the Sadducees did not believe in the resurrection of the dead. For them, death meant the party was over. This question was a bit of a ruse.

"In the resurrection whose wife will she be? For the seven had married her."

Why would they ask a question about the resurrection they did not believe in? In their minds, this complicated riddle of a question would expose not only Jesus' faith in the resurrection of the dead but also its absurdity. Jesus sees straight through them and indicts them for their bad exegesis (method of interpreting Scripture) and chides them for their lack of faith in the power of God.

Jesus said to them, "Is not this the reason you are wrong, that you know neither the scriptures nor the power of God?"

First, Jesus gives an authoritative word about the resurrection of the dead and marriage. Bottom line? Marriage ends with death. In the resurrection there will be no marriage. There is a much larger covenant at work within which the covenant of marriage is controlled. The covenant between God and his people supersedes the covenant of marriage. It outlasts it. Next he takes on their biblical interpretation by citing a covenant-oriented text he knew they embraced, Exodus 3:6. It's the burning bush story when God says to Moses, "I am the God of your father, the God of Abraham, the God of Isaac, and the God of Jacob."

My sources make an interesting case for Jesus' application of this text. It goes like this. In this covenant affirmation, God affirms his faithfulness to Abraham, Isaac, and Jacob, which is a covenant that transcends death. Of what worth would it all be if only for the infinitesimally short period of time in which a person is alive on this earth? This God has power over sin and death. God is a God of the living and in his kingdom, though people die because of the curse of sin, yet shall they live because of the promise of resurrection. Jesus then rebukes with these words: "*You are quite wrong.*"

It's probably as close as he will come to calling someone an idiot. He's telling them that their big problem is they don't believe what they believe. In other words, if you believe in the God of Abraham, Isaac, and Jacob, you believe in the resurrection of the dead. You don't get one without the other.

Moving this forward a couple of thousand years, let's ask ourselves this question: Do I believe in the resurrection of the dead? I've said it ten thousand times in the Apostles' Creed, "I believe in the Holy Spirit, the Holy catholic Church, the communion of saints, the forgiveness of sins, *the resurrection of the body*, and the life everlasting."

Over the past couple hundred years, we have mostly bought stock in the idea of an ethereal heaven where disembodied spirits enjoy the presence of God and loved ones who have gone before—you know, the better place we reference when a person dies. I don't want to diminish anyone's faith in the immediacy of being in the presence of God at one's death. After all, Paul clearly said to be absent from the body is to be present with the Lord (see 2 Corinthians 5:6). I do want to say heaven as we commonly conceive of it is not the long view. The long game is the resurrection of the body and the life everlasting. The long view isn't heaven; it's earth—as in "on earth as it is in heaven."

The resurrection of the body is our core faith. As Paul also said,

> For if the dead are not raised, then Christ has not been raised either. And if Christ has not been raised, your faith is futile; you are still in your sins. Then those also who have fallen asleep in Christ are lost. If only for this life we have hope in Christ, we are of all people most to be pitied. (1 Cor. 15:16–19)

The resurrection of the body is the long view. Permit me an emphatic declaration of biblical faith: Jesus' bodily resurrection means our bodily resurrection or it means nothing. If we do not believe in the resurrection of the body, whatever it is that we believe about the resurrection of Jesus is something other than the Christian faith—"the faith that was once for all entrusted to the saints" (Jude 3 NRSV).

The Prayer

Spirit of the living God, fall afresh on me.

The Questions

- Do you believe in the resurrection of the dead? Is it core to your faith or peripheral?

- What difference might taking the long view have in your everyday life?

The Two Ways of Keeping the Law and Why It Matters Most

MARK 12:28–34 | One of the teachers of the law came and heard them debating. Noticing that Jesus had given them a good answer, he asked him, "Of all the commandments, which is the most important?"

"The most important one," answered Jesus, "is this: 'Hear, O Israel: The Lord our God, the Lord is one. Love the Lord your God with all your heart and with all your soul and with all your mind and with all your strength.' The second is this: 'Love your neighbor as yourself.' There is no commandment greater than these."

"Well said, teacher," the man replied. "You are right in saying that God is one and there is no other but him. To love him with all your heart, with all your understanding and with all your strength, and to love your neighbor as yourself is more important than all burnt offerings and sacrifices."

When Jesus saw that he had answered wisely, he said to him, "You are not far from the kingdom of God." And from then on no one dared ask him any more questions.

Consider This

There are 613 individual laws together accounted for the Law. We are back to Final Jeopardy, with another major question: Of all the 613 laws, which one was the greatest?

What is Law all about anyway? When you have fallen human beings in the same vicinity, laws become necessary. The essence of fallenness is selfishness. It consists in a person's inability to see beyond themselves to others. In its raw form, human fallenness leads to a complete and utter inability to recognize and respect the boundaries of other people (consider theft, murder, and adultery, for starters). This creates chaos. Laws delineate order.

The Law intentions to train fallen people to see, respect, and come to revere the sacred worth of other people. Stepping outside of the biblical context, take speed limit laws, for example. Speed limits aim to protect people from one another. So why do I speed? I speed because I think my need to get where I want to go outweighs the similar needs of other people. I disregard their needs and their safety in the interest of advancing my own self-interest. For me, observing the speed limit has nothing to do with preserving the security of others and everything to do with me not getting a ticket. Speed limit laws aspire to train me in placing the safety needs of others on the road ahead of my need to beat the yellow light. Unfortunately, speed limit laws are powerless when it comes to changing my orientation around other people.

I think it's why Jesus chose this commandment as the most important:

"The most important one," answered Jesus, "is this: 'Hear, O Israel: The Lord our God, the Lord is one. Love the Lord your God with all your heart and with all your soul and with all your mind and with all your strength.' The second is this: 'Love your neighbor as yourself.' There is no commandment greater than these."

You see, I can keep the speed limit laws to perfection, yet my efforts could be completely self-serving and have nothing to do with anyone else's well-being. This is why Jesus cites the law of holy love. One cannot keep the holy law of love without it being about other people. To keep the law of holy love of God and neighbor implies and requires me to get beyond myself and into the realm of serving others for their sake.

When Jesus raised this command to the status of the most important commandment he essentially said, "This law of the holy love of God and neighbor is the whole tamale. The rest is just commentary."

Discipleship designs to liberate us from the bondage of ourselves freeing us to give ourselves to others. One of the most simple and practical everyday ways I can give myself to others just might be slowing down and driving the speed limit. I am not that mature at the moment. It's got me asking a lot of other questions of myself. Is the fundamental orientation of my obedience about protecting myself, my image, my reputation, and my stuff? Or is the fundamental orientation of my obedience about protecting others. If I'm honest, I'm not thinking one whit about the strangers in the cars all

It is Not about Me —

around me. I don't want to cause a wreck, but then that's about me too.

Some famous theologian once said something to this effect, "The Law was given so that the grace of the Holy Spirit might be desired. And the grace of the Holy Spirit was given so that the Law might be truly obeyed."

Again, today's laws and the biblical law are not the same thing, but I do see some of the same governing dynamics crossing the chasm between then and now.

What about your posture toward the laws of our everyday lives? Is that about observing the law for your own sake or have you reached a place where observing the law is for the sake of others? That's what the greatest commandment is all about: liberating the law from self-serving observance into the light of the love of God and others. This could change everything. I'll be thinking about that on my drive to work today.

The Prayer

Spirit of the living God, fall afresh on me.

The Questions

- Is keeping the law (or not) about yourself or others?
- How does this line of thinking reshape your understanding of law? Of love? Of God? Of neighbor?

Moving from Information to Conversation

MARK 12:35–40 ESV | And as Jesus taught in the temple, he said, "How can the scribes say that the Christ is the son of David? David himself, in the Holy Spirit, declared,

"'The Lord said to my Lord,
"Sit at my right hand,
  until I put your enemies under your feet.'"

David himself calls him Lord. So how is he his son?" And the great throng heard him gladly.

And in his teaching he said, "Beware of the scribes, who like to walk around in long robes and like greetings in the market-places and have the best seats in the synagogues and the places of honor at feasts, who devour widows' houses and for a pretense make long prayers. They will receive the greater condemnation."

Consider This

I recently sat at one of those long tables found in some Starbucks coffee shops, one of those kind where different people come and go. Some sit at the table and mind their own business. Others come with a friend or two and sit across from each other and visit. Still others will strike up a conversation with complete strangers who are also sitting at the table. It's a curious social convention.

On my recent visit, two men came and took seats across from each other just down the table from me. They were close enough where I could listen in without much difficulty. It became obvious that one of the men was mentoring the other in the Christian faith. They both had their Bibles opened on the table. The discussion quickly turned to monologue as the older man proceeded to "teach" the younger man for an almost thirty-minute stretch. He talked *at* him. I observed as the younger man tried to interject with his questions to no avail. It proved to be a discipleship adventure in missing the point.

One of the things I appreciate about today's text has to do with just this point. Jesus was in a teaching mode in the temple. Around him were a number of people who recognized his authority. Jesus, of course, was an expert regarding the texts he was teaching on. He knew precisely what they meant. However, two small words stand out in the text, which show both his respect for people and the humility of his discipleship craft. See if you can pick out the two words.

And as Jesus taught in the temple, he [asked], "How can the scribes say that the Christ is the son of David?"

Did you spot them? The two words are, "he [asked]." Did he ask because he didn't know? Of course not. I think he asked because it was a challenging conundrum. Put in my own context it would be like asking how my own son could be my God. Often when I know the answer to a difficult question I like to demonstrate my expertise in preemptively answering. I prefer the ease of what I call the download method. It's what that man next to me at Starbucks was doing. He down-loaded a ton of biblical content on his mentee. The download method tends to be an informational approach.

The process of making disciples of Jesus Christ requires a conversational ethic rather than an informational approach. We communicate *with* others rather than talking *to* them or worse, *at* them. It's never occurred to me, but at the core of the word "communicate" is the word "commune." When we commune with another person, it's about a lot more than passing on information. It implies a rich dimension of sharing in a context of humble fellowship. It's a participation in mutual exploration. It's got me thinking. I don't want to be "The Bible Answer Guy" even if I have some answers. I want to learn to ask good questions.

In my experience, the people who understand the Bible the best aren't necessarily those who have acquired the most information about it. They are the people who have learned to ask the best questions.

I know today's text likely didn't intend to make the point I'm making. Admittedly, it's a tangential observation. The text is all about Jesus trying to help his followers understand that his agenda could not be framed from a mere human-oriented approach to national sovereignty (i.e., restoring the Davidic throne). Jesus was not bringing a geopolitical solution, but an eternal kingdom. You just can't download that on people. It has to be revealed to them. Asking questions causes people to lean into a conversation rather than away. It opens them up to receive revelation.

The Prayer

Spirit of the living God, fall afresh on me.

The Questions

- What keeps you from asking questions in a conversation when you already know the answer? When you don't?
- How might you approach conversations differently today, especially ones about faith?

66 When Two Cents Is Worth More than a Million Dollars

MARK 12:41–44 NRSV | He sat down opposite the treasury, and watched the crowd putting money into the treasury. Many rich people put in large sums. A poor widow came and put in two small copper coins, which are worth a penny. Then he called his disciples and said to them, "Truly I tell you, this poor widow has put in more than all those who are contributing to the treasury. For all of them have contributed out of their abundance; but she out of her poverty has put in everything she had, all she had to live on."

Consider This

Two copper coins are more than very large offerings of money. How can this be? How can 2/8 of a cent be more than $1,000? It makes no sense. How can the least be the greatest and the last be the first? How does the smallest seed become the largest tree? How does humility lead to exaltation?

None of this makes any sense and yet it makes perfect sense to Jesus. So if it doesn't make sense to me, then I have not yet learned to think like Jesus. The world's way of thinking and its value system is more often than not completely opposite of Jesus' way of thinking and value system.

> For the message of the cross is foolishness to those who are perishing, but to us who are being saved it is the power of God. . . . For the foolishness of God is wiser than human wisdom, and the weakness of God is stronger than human strength. (1 Cor. 1:18, 25)

Faith means learning to trust the wisdom and values of Jesus even though it seems completely opposite of the ways of the world. When Jesus says the widow has put in more than all of the wealthy people who clearly put in more money, then the widow has put in more. It gets even more interesting when we remember the previous text; the one just preceding this story about the widow. I'll refresh our memory:

> As he taught, Jesus said, "Watch out for the teachers of the law. They like to walk around in flowing robes and be greeted with respect in the marketplaces, and

> have the most important seats in the synagogues and
> the places of honor at banquets. They devour widows'
> houses and for a show make lengthy prayers. These
> men will be punished most severely." (Mark 12:38–40)

Do you see what he's saying? It's so easy for us to think we get this concept about the most respected people being the most despicable, but we don't. Jesus' analogy is not to the crooked politicians of our time, but more likely the people in our communities who are most esteemed and respected. I'm just hoping he's not talking about me.

If there's one thing I've become sure of in life it's this: however things seems to be on the outside, you can bet that they're not really that way. Faith means living in the midst of the world's value system with a completely different set of values, a different mind-set. When the world's compass points south, we can bet Jesus' compass points north. However, discipleship is not about just opposing the values of the world and trying to do the opposite. Discipleship is about following Jesus—exclusively—when it makes sense to us and when it doesn't. Discipleship is the process of being trained by the indwelling Holy Spirit to put on the mind of Christ.

There's a text in Scripture that has perhaps become more important to me than any other text. It's one I have remembered and I try and rehearse it every day. I commend it to you. I want to encourage you to give yourself to learning this text forward and backward, inside-out and upside-down.

In your relationships with one another, have the same mindset as Christ Jesus: Who, being in very nature God, did not consider equality with God something to be used to his own advantage; rather, he made himself nothing by taking the very nature of a servant, being made in human likeness.

And being found in appearance as a man, he humbled himself by becoming obedient to death— even death on a cross!

Therefore God exalted him to the highest place and gave him the name that is above every name, that at the name of Jesus every knee should bow, in heaven and on earth and under the earth, and every tongue acknowledge that Jesus Christ is Lord, to the glory of God the Father. (Phil. 2:5–11)

It's only as we grow in the very mind of Jesus that we will ever hope to truly understand how two cents can be worth more than a million dollars.

The Prayer

Spirit of the living God, fall afresh on me.

The Questions

- Have you ever done something that made no sense in the terms and value system of the world and yet seemed to be the wisdom of God and the way of Jesus? How did it turn out?

67 When It's Time to Build Something More than Buildings

MARK 13:1–2 | As Jesus was leaving the temple, one of his disciples said to him, "Look, Teacher! What massive stones! What magnificent buildings!"

"Do you see all these great buildings?" replied Jesus. "Not one stone here will be left on another; every one will be thrown down."

Consider This

"Look, Teacher! What massive stones! What magnificent buildings!"

The human race has defined itself by its buildings. We love building projects. From the ancient Ziggurats of the Mayan people to the massive Egyptian pyramids to the great Taj Mahal in India to the Colosseum and Pantheon in Rome to the Acropolis in Athens, the human race has defined itself by its building projects.

Far from an ancient thing, this practice continues to the present day. America is symbolized by its great buildings, from the United States Capitol to the White House to the massive marble memorials. It's fascinating how the radical Islamic terrorist Osama bin Laden launched his attack not so much against people but against the most symbolic buildings in our country. (To be clear, he intended to effect mass casualties.) And, in the case of this national tragedy, it turned out it wasn't our buildings that defined us after all.

Today's text proves the point yet again. The temple had become more important to the people than the God for whom the temple was built. And therein lies the problem with buildings. We unwittingly turn them into idols. The prophet Jeremiah had something to say about that.

> This is the word that came to Jeremiah from the LORD: "Stand at the gate of the LORD's house and there proclaim this message:
>
> "'Hear the word of the LORD, all you people of Judah who come through these gates to worship the LORD. This is what the LORD Almighty, the God of Israel, says: Reform your ways and your actions, and I will let you live in this place. Do not trust in deceptive words and say, "This is the temple of the LORD, the temple of the LORD, the temple of the LORD!" If you really change your ways and your actions and deal with each other justly, if you do not oppress the foreigner, the fatherless or the widow and do not shed innocent blood in this place, and if you do not follow other gods to your own harm, then I will let you live in this place, in the land I gave your ancestors for ever and ever. But look, you are trusting in deceptive words that are worthless.
>
> "'Will you steal and murder, commit adultery and perjury, burn incense to Baal and follow other gods you have not known, and then come and stand before

me in this house, which bears my Name, and say, "We
are safe"—safe to do all these detestable things? Has
this house, which bears my Name, become a den of
robbers to you? But I have been watching! declares the
LORD.'" (Jer. 7:1–11)

Days after his cleansing visit to the temple, here's how
Jesus put it: *"Do you see all these great buildings?" replied
Jesus. "Not one stone here will be left on another; every one
will be thrown down."*

And with stunning accuracy, less than forty years later,
it happened. Every stone was thrown down by the Roman
armies in AD 70.

I'm convinced there's a word in here for the contemporary
church. It's fascinating how much we make of church buildings here in North America. To be sure, they serve marvelous
purposes and much good comes from them, but they are not
the church. Despite that, just about anytime anyone speaks
of going to the church they are referring to a building. All too
often, our buildings have come to define our churches.

When people speak of a church in many parts of the world,
the last thing they are talking about is a building. They are
referring to a small group of men and women who have
staked their lives on the Word of God and pledged their faith
to follow Jesus.

A similar thing might be said about our own houses and
the way we confuse our houses with our homes. Anyone who
has built a house knows how easy it is to not keep the main
thing the main thing. In the wake of disastrous storms or

fires or other natural disasters that decimate peoples' houses the story is always the same. They are sad about the loss of all their earthly belongings, but at the same time they are awakened and clinging to what matters most—each other—and they stand in awe of the mercy that spared their lives. When it becomes all about the building instead of what the building was built for, we may be headed for trouble.

The Prayer

Spirit of the living God, fall afresh on me.

The Questions

- What is it about us that wants to define ourselves by our buildings? What would it look like to invest our lives into other lives more than into buildings?

On the Day It All Hits the Fan and the Day after That

MARK 13:3–11 ESV | And as he sat on the Mount of Olives opposite the temple, Peter and James and John and Andrew asked him privately, "Tell us, when will these things be, and what will be the sign when all these things are about to be accomplished?" And Jesus began to say to them, "See that no one leads you astray. Many will come in my name, saying, 'I

am he!' and they will lead many astray. And when you hear of wars and rumors of wars, do not be alarmed. This must take place, but the end is not yet. For nation will rise against nation, and kingdom against kingdom. There will be earthquakes in various places; there will be famines. These are but the beginning of the birth pains.

"But be on your guard. For they will deliver you over to councils, and you will be beaten in synagogues, and you will stand before governors and kings for my sake, to bear witness before them. And the gospel must first be proclaimed to all nations. And when they bring you to trial and deliver you over, do not be anxious beforehand what you are to say, but say whatever is given you in that hour, for it is not you who speak, but the Holy Spirit."

Consider This

It was one of those conversations for the ages. Jesus and four alarmed disciples sat atop the ancient Mount of Olives gazing across the Kidron Valley at the majesty of the magnificent temple. In a stunned silence, they tried to wrap their minds around the unthinkable: that the temple, this enduring monument to their favored national identity and the focal point of their faith, would be decimated in ruins. They had moved from if to when.

"Tell us, when will these things be, and what will be the sign when all these things are about to be accomplished?"

All their hopes lived in Jesus Messiah, the One who would reinstate the sovereignty of God in the land, restore the kingdom, expel the infidels of Rome, and usher in an era of unprecedented peace and prosperity. They probably saw Jesus' raucous rumble in the temple as the pre-game warm-up; a flexing of messianic muscle. They had no category for a post-Jesus, post-temple Israel. The whole thing seemed to be coming apart at the seams, unraveling before their very eyes.

It's not a fitting analogy, but for example's sake, imagine the United States of America not only ravaged by terrorists, but ruled by them. Imagine the complete destruction of the Capitol building and the White House and the great memorials. It is so unthinkable, it's impossible to imagine. And there isn't even a word to describe the prospect of imagining what would happen beyond that.

Jesus is talking to his disciples not only about the unthinkable day when it would all come down, but worse, the unimaginable day after that. Now, note what he says to them. In my understanding and way of thinking about it, he told them something akin to the following:

> You are about to find yourselves at the tip of the spear of the movement of my gospel, which will not stop until it reaches every nation on the planet. The Holy Spirit is going to carry you to places you never dreamed of going. At times, you will find yourselves on the wrong side of a prison door. At other times, you will find yourselves standing before the thrones of kings. Do not be afraid. You answer only to the King of kings. The world will seem to literally fall apart all around you, but do not be afraid. You will be following

the trail of the One who will in fact be making all things new. The forces of sin and death and evil will be unrelenting in their pursuit of you, but do not be afraid. You will be standing on the shoulders of a Messiah who has defeated the rule of sin and destroyed the reign of death. The days ahead will be painstakingly hard, but they will be wholeheartedly glorious.

Here's the good news: I've got this, and you've got me and everywhere you go I will establish my kingdom and build my church, and the gates of hell don't stand a chance. No weapon formed against this gospel will prosper. All who rise up against it will fall down. Be warned though: nothing is going to happen like you expected it to happen, and you will thank me later. For it will only be in the wake of the death of your expectations that the future of my making can break through. Let go of your expectations so that a deeper expectancy might be birthed. Let go of your fears and take hold of me. Let go of your control and take up my cross. All of your training and experience has brought you to this place where you hold nothing but possess everything. You are on the eve of a future you could never in a million years look ahead and predict, and it will lead to looking back on a past you would never in a million years change. Be on your guard. Don't be alarmed. And never be afraid.

I don't mean to put words in Jesus' mouth and, to be sure, I make absolutely no claim that he ever said what I've written.

That said, I do think this is the kind of thing he would say. I think this is the kind of thing he was saying in the days leading up to the cross and in those pre-dawn days of Pentecost. Frankly, I think it's the same kind of thing he may be saying to his church throughout the world, and perhaps in a timely way, to the church in America. Finally, I think it's the kind of thing he may be saying to many of you today. So take it and test it. Perhaps there's a word of prophecy tucked in there somewhere for you.

Wherever the systems, securities, structures, and where-withal of the world as we know it is coming apart at the seams, you can bet the kingdom of God is coming together at its core.

The Prayer
Spirit of the living God, fall afresh on me.

The Questions
- Are you holding on to a limiting set of expectations that could be holding you back from the expectancy of the transcendent possibilities of God?
- What would it mean to begin letting those expectations go?

69 Why We Must Leave behind *Left Behind*

MARK 13:12–19 NRSV | "Brother will betray brother to death, and a father his child, and children will rise against parents and have them put to death; and you will be hated by all because of my name. But the one who endures to the end will be saved.

"But when you see the desolating sacrilege set up where it ought not to be (let the reader understand), then those in Judea must flee to the mountains; the one on the housetop must not go down or enter the house to take anything away; the one in the field must not turn back to get a coat. Woe to those who are pregnant and to those who are nursing infants in those days! Pray that it may not be in winter. For in those days there will be suffering, such as has not been from the beginning of the creation that God created until now, no, and never will be."

Consider This

This passage of Scripture we find ourselves in the midst of these past couple of days and the next couple to come is extremely challenging to understand.

As a result, I will not attempt to speak beyond my own understanding of the text at this point in my life and discipleship. I will handle such things as "the abomination that causes desolation" when I gain a better grasp on it.

Here's what I understand and the kind of application I think the text of recent and future days has for us today. At the risk of overgeneralizing, I will be short and to the point.

From the first century to the twenty-first century and every year of every century in between, we have witnessed the people of God moving in one of two directions with respect to the future. They gravitate toward either an apocalyptic or an eschatological outlook on the future. So, what's the difference?

Apocalypticism tends to focus on doom, destruction, and disaster. Eschatology tends to focus on ultimate outcomes and the framework of the last things. Apocalypticism breeds fear and anxiety. On the other hand, good eschatology fosters the fruit of hope. Let's be clear. Good eschatology does not mean optimism. Eschatology must be truthful about the future. It will not be easy. There will be hardship and pain and difficulty, but there is a greater reality being born right in the midst of it all. Apocalypticism keeps our focus on all the signs of impending doom. Eschatology focuses our vision on God and the glorious things to come.

Jesus gives his disciples the truth about the challenges that lay ahead, but he paints a much bigger picture of the greater things in the making. In fact, he commands us to fix our eyes on the future in such a way that it impacts every decision we make in the present. He is leading us toward a future that inspires nobility, faith, courage, and love in the face of despairing conditions and seemingly impossible scenarios.

In every age, many God-fearing Christian voices spread their apocalyptic anxiety like a cancer among the people.

It fosters fear-mongering and it brings out the worst in the church. They tend to be the louder voices. In every age, there are unfortunately fewer followers of Jesus who catch a glimpse of the beatific vision—the beautiful and glorious vision of the coming kingdom of God. These tend to be the quieter, yet more powerful leaders of the faith. Apocalyptic anxiety sells books and blockbuster movie tickets. Eschatological hope steels faith and emboldens holy love.

When I think about the great creeds of the church, they are filled with eschatological hope. Yes, we confess a final judgment but also the communion of saints, the forgiveness of sins, the resurrection of the body, and the life everlasting!

The Prayer

Spirit of the living God, fall afresh on me.

The Questions

- On the spectrum of apocalyptic anxiety to eschatological hope, where do you land?
- The only way our anxiety can be starved is to feed it with real hope. What might that look like for you today?

70 | When the Sky Starts Falling

MARK 13:20–26 | "If the Lord had not cut short those days, no one would survive. But for the sake of the elect, whom he has chosen, he has shortened them. At that time if anyone says to you, 'Look, here is the Messiah!' or, 'Look, there he is!' do not believe it. For false messiahs and false prophets will appear and perform signs and wonders to deceive, if possible, even the elect. So be on your guard; I have told you everything ahead of time.

"But in those days, following that distress,

"'the sun will be darkened,
and the moon will not give its light;
the stars will fall from the sky,
and the heavenly bodies will be shaken.'

"At that time people will see the Son of Man coming in clouds with great power and glory. And he will send his angels and gather his elect from the four winds, from the ends of the earth to the ends of the heavens."

Consider This

You may remember from yesterday we articulated the difference between apocalyptic anxiety and eschatological hope. Those are definitely some twenty-five-dollar words, and probably not suitable for casual conversation, but we need them for the sake of our conversation.

What's important to note here is that Jesus is giving us a sequence of events, but no time line. Here's where all the apocalyptic confusion comes into play. Do you see the difference? When leaders take the sequence Jesus offers and turn it into an actual time line, we get into trouble. With respect to time lines, Jesus made it abundantly clear. Just a few verses later he says this: "But about that day or hour no one knows, not even the angels in heaven, nor the Son, but only the Father" (Mark 13:32).

Following his resurrection and just prior to his ascension he put it this way: "Then they gathered around him and asked him, 'Lord, are you at this time going to restore the kingdom to Israel?' He said to them: 'It is not for you to know the times or dates the Father has set by his own authority'" (Acts 1:6–7).

In Mark 13, when Jesus speaks about the coming tribulation and impending disaster, he is prophesying concerning the destruction of the temple, which would happen some forty years later. The best I can understand, he did not intend to connect his return to that event. The destruction of the temple would signify in a final way that the presence of the Lord had left the building. The location of the presence of the Lord in the world would be in the body of Christ, with Jesus as its head.

That Jesus Christ will return to the earth is an irrefutable fact of our faith. When he will return is an unknowable reality. In the scheme and sequence of things, while we can't know the timing, we can know that when the things listed below begin to happen, his return is imminent.

"But in those days, following that distress, 'the sun will be darkened, and the moon will not give its light; the stars will fall from the sky, and the heavenly bodies will be shaken.' At that time people will see the Son of Man coming in clouds with great power and glory."

Until that time, we will see all sorts of tribulation and trials. We will see many versions of false prophets and would-be messianic leaders. People will insist on reading these signs as direct proof of the impending return of Jesus. It will stir up all sorts of unnecessary apocalyptic anxiety. Meanwhile, we can stand firm in our faith, filled with the hope of the gospel, and bank on the certainty of his return. And when the sun and the moon go dark and stars start falling from the skies, then we can start looking to the clouds and getting ready for the great celebration of the wedding of the Lamb.

"The sky is falling!" That's the essence of apocalyptic anxiety. But the truth is, the sky will one day fall. We don't need to fear that. We only need to be ready and to help as many people as we possibly can to be ready with us. When the sky does fall, it will not be something someone has to announce. It will be apparent. In the end, the beauty of the falling sky will be the coming of Jesus on the descending clouds. It will be a good day.

This is my best wisdom on the text, and while I stand by it without adding any disclaimers, I may be wrong.

The Prayer

Spirit of the living God, fall afresh on me.

The Questions

- Is it enough to have a grasp of the sequence of things without knowing the timing? What is it about us that needs to know everything before it happens?

71 Why Does the Word of God Endure Forever?

MARK 13:28–31 ESV | "From the fig tree learn its lesson: as soon as its branch becomes tender and puts out its leaves, you know that summer is near. So also, when you see these things taking place, you know that he is near, at the very gates. Truly, I say to you, this generation will not pass away until all these things take place. Heaven and earth will pass away, but my words will not pass away."

Consider This

As we near the end of this, the final speech of Jesus in the Gospel of Mark, it's worth remembering how it all got started.

> As Jesus was leaving the temple, one of his disciples said to him, "Look, Teacher! What massive stones! What magnificent buildings!" "Do you see all these great buildings?" replied Jesus. "Not one stone here will be left on another; every one will be thrown down." As Jesus was sitting on the Mount of Olives opposite the temple, Peter, James, John and Andrew asked him privately, "Tell us, when will these things happen? And what will be the sign that they are all about to be fulfilled?" (Mark 13:1–4)

This little contextual clue—"When will these things happen?"—could save a lot of apocalyptic angst. Right up to today's text, Jesus is responding to the disciples' question about the destruction of the temple. He is not talking about the end of time. This is what the fig tree analogy is all about—understanding and interpreting the signs that indicate the imminent end of Jerusalem as they knew it.

So if this was all about the destruction of the temple in the first century, what on earth does it have to do with us? Nothing and everything. I think the clue is in the next and closing verses from today's text.

"Truly, I say to you, this generation will not pass away until all these things take place. Heaven and earth will pass away, but my words will not pass away."

Jesus nailed it with his prophecy about the temple. The temple was brutally destroyed in AD 70. It happened in that very generation. On the day Jesus made the prophecy, no one in their right mind would have ever imagined the magnificent temple would come down. Jesus knew. All these years later, his words still stand. They witness to us of an event in history that has little bearing on our everyday lives, yet it has everything to do with it. Jesus' words will never pass away. Everything Jesus said has been tested and it can be trusted. The words of Jesus offer the only ultimate security in existence. Everything else will pass away. World history proves it out. Consider how so many of the great societies and civilizations in the history of the world today lie in ruins. They have passed away and all that keeps them alive are the words of the tour guides. All the words of countless great and powerful leaders have all but passed away. They are recorded in books and taught in universities, but they are not alive. The teachings of the Buddha and Muhammad and Moroni continue to be treasured and revered by many, but they are as alive as the pages on which they are written.

The Word of God stands in a category of its own. The Word of God is living and active because the God of the Word is living and active. The words of Jesus will never pass away because Jesus will never pass away.

"*Heaven and earth will pass away, but my words will not pass away.*"

A lot of people have wasted a lot of time trying to dismantle, deconstruct, and demythologize the words of Jesus, many of them self-avowed Christians with good intentions while others were satanic emissaries straight from hell. Their work and words always find their way to the ash heap of history. Those who stake their lives on the indestructible words of Jesus, though they die, yet shall they live and leave a legacy that lives on.

How about taking those thirteen words, "Heaven and earth will pass away, but my words will not pass away," and making them your mantra this week. Here's a practical prompt: Anytime you begin to read anything whether it be online or on paper, recall these words and say them aloud: "The grass withers and the flowers fall, but the word of our God endures forever" (Isa. 40:8).

The Prayer

Spirit of the living God, fall afresh on me.

The Questions

- Have you reckoned with the indestructibility of the words of Jesus? How are they becoming the substance and source of your life?

Why Being Ready for the End Means Being Joyfully Alive in the Present

72

MARK 13:32–37 NRSV | "But about that day or hour no one knows, neither the angels in heaven, nor the Son, but only the Father. Beware, keep alert; for you do not know when the time will come. It is like a man going on a journey, when he leaves home and puts his slaves in charge, each with his work, and commands the doorkeeper to be on the watch. Therefore, keep awake—for you do not know when the master of the house will come, in the evening, or at midnight, or at cockcrow, or at dawn, or else he may find you asleep when he comes suddenly. And what I say to you I say to all: Keep awake."

Consider This

And so we come to the end of Jesus' teaching about what it means to be prepared for the future. Let's summarize.

Jesus speaks of two distinct outcomes. First, is the coming destruction of the temple and Jerusalem. He gives ample signs and even something of a time line relating to its occurrence: "Even so, when you see these things happening, you know that it is near, right at the door. Truly I tell you, this generation will certainly not pass away until all these things have happened" (Mark 13:29–30).

Second, is the end of the age and the return of the Lord. Today's text makes clear that there is no time line and there will be no signs or warnings.

"Therefore, keep awake—for you do not know when the master of the house will come, in the evening, or at midnight, or at cockcrow, or at dawn, or else he may find you asleep when he comes suddenly."

Because we cannot know, our remedy is to be prepared and the essence of being prepared does not mean storing up water and food. Being prepared means staying vigilant, alert, and expectant. It means cultivating a lifestyle of attentiveness to the presence of God in all things. It does not mean an anxiety-ridden fretting away of the present while looking ahead to the future. To be attentive is to live completely, wholeheartedly, and joyfully alive to the Father, abiding in the life of Jesus through the gift of the Holy Spirit.

Watchfulness—living attentive to and alive in the presence of God—this is why we constantly pray and consistently fast and daily feast on the Word of God. We meet Jesus here.

Watchfulness—living attentive to and alive in the presence of God—this is why we meet regularly as the body of Christ around his table to remember and proclaim the Lord's death and resurrection until he comes. We meet Jesus here.

Watchfulness—living attentive to and alive in the presence of God—this is why we band together with a few other believers to watch over one another in love, encouragement, and accountability. We meet Jesus here.

Watchfulness—living attentive to and alive in the presence of God—this is why we feed the hungry and clothe the naked and care for the sick and welcome the stranger and visit the imprisoned. We meet Jesus here.

These are not so many spiritual disciplines and good deeds we ought to be doing. This is not a lifestyle of religious duty. This is life. These are the divinely appointed ways and means to live and move and have our being in the presence of the God who made us and who remakes us because he loves us.

Do you see how far this way of life is from apocalyptic anxiety? This is the way of eschatological hope. Far from fear and sadness, this is all about hope and gladness. In the face of the worst day of our life, this is the faith that makes our soul well. It's why Horatio Spafford wrote the song, "It Is Well with My Soul": "And Lord, haste the day that my faith becomes sight, the clouds be rolled back as a scroll; the trump shall resound, and the Lord shall descend, even so, it is well with my soul."

Tomorrow we shift gears from last things to the ultimate thing, which is the suffering, death, and resurrection of our Lord Jesus Christ. This holy calling of Jesus creates a most appropriate bridge from chapter 13 to chapter 14.

"And what I say to you I say to all: Keep awake."

Let's take this holy calling with us and let's go singing, "It is well. It is well with my soul."

The Prayer

Spirit of the living God, fall afresh on me.

The Questions

- Have you made (or are you making) the shift from so many obligatory religious duties to this way of living attentive and alive in the presence of God?
- Do you see how prayer can be more about divine presence than dutiful practice? How fasting can be more about divine fellowship than just gritting your teeth and doing it?
- Do you see how attentiveness to those in need can be more about divine encounter than having pity on poor people?

73 The Three Kinds of People You Meet on the Way to the Cross

MARK 14:1–5 | Now the Passover and the Festival of Unleavened Bread were only two days away, and the chief priests and the teachers of the law were scheming to arrest Jesus secretly and kill him. "But not during the festival," they said, "or the people may riot."

While he was in Bethany, reclining at the table in the home of Simon the Leper, a woman came with an alabaster jar of very expensive perfume, made of pure nard. She broke the jar and poured the perfume on his head.

Some of those present were saying indignantly to one another, "Why this waste of perfume? It could have been sold for more than a year's wages and the money given to the poor." And they rebuked her harshly.

Consider This

As we make the turn to the cross, today's text (and tomorrow's) shows us the three basic kinds of people we will meet on the way—then and now.

Type #1: The people who are concerned about maintaining their power: *and the chief priests and the teachers of the law were scheming to arrest Jesus secretly and kill him.*

Type #2: The people who are concerned about maintaining their reputation: *Some of those present were saying indignantly to one another, "Why this waste of perfume? It could have been sold for more than a year's wages and the money given to the poor." And they rebuked her harshly.*

Type #3: The people who are concerned neither about their power or their reputation but who actually lay down their power in order to preserve the reputation of another: *a woman came with an alabaster jar of very expensive perfume, made of pure nard. She broke the jar and poured the perfume on his head.*

The Type #1 people are deadly. The Type #2 people are dedicated. The Type #3 people are devoted.

These three kinds of people are always present.

The Type #1 people are always present. Look for the people who seemingly have the most to lose in a situation. They are the power players. They play hardball. They are law makers and law enforcers and, ironically, they turn out to be law breakers. Relative to the other two types, there are far fewer Type #1 people.

The Type #2 people abound. They are everywhere. They don't make the rules, but they will bend over backward to follow them. However, in following the rules, they often miss the point even though they technically get it right. These are the dedicated and disciplined disciples. Type #2 people are often well-intentioned, good people. Ironically, they can be the most dangerous people of all. They tend to put principle over people.

The Type #3 people are extremely rare. For them it's all about people. They are about people in ways that redefine principle and power in the light of holy love. They are uncalculated givers. They do inconceivable things in the interest of loving God and others. In fact, they have such a level of self-awareness of their gratitude that they become self-forgetful about their own needs. They are the ones whose life makes no sense apart from Jesus. He is their only explanation and, because of him, their lives are arresting. They are the unlikely holy ones, whose lives may seem small and inconsequential at the time, but who will never be forgotten. They are the worshippers.

The Prayer

Spirit of the living God, fall afresh on me.

The Questions

- Can you see yourself in any of these three types of people?
- What simple step might you take today toward becoming a Type #3 person?

The Big Problem with Being More Dedicated to God

74

MARK 14:6–11 ESV | But Jesus said, "Leave her alone. Why do you trouble her? She has done a beautiful thing to me. For you always have the poor with you, and whenever you want, you can do good for them. But you will not always have me. She has done what she could; she has anointed my body beforehand for burial. And truly, I say to you, wherever the gospel is proclaimed in the whole world, what she has done will be told in memory of her."

Then Judas Iscariot, who was one of the twelve, went to the chief priests in order to betray him to them. And when they heard it, they were glad and promised to give him money. And he sought an opportunity to betray him.

Consider This

Remember our discussion yesterday about the three kinds of people you meet on the way to the cross? In case not, here's a quick rehash: the Type #1 people are deadly; the Type #2 people are dedicated; the Type #3 people are devoted.

So where would you land Judas in this mix?

If you said Type #1 you are wrong. Judas was Type #2. He was a dedicated and trusted disciple of Jesus; we are told in another of the Gospel accounts that he actually kept up with the money for the whole group. Judas was a first-round draft pick—one of the Twelve. He was dedicated to the cause. Some believe Judas was actually trying to foment the revolution by turning Jesus in; that he knew doing this would force the battle. We may never know.

This is where the deception of "dedication" comes into play. My theory is this: my dedication is really all about me and my effort and my commitment. And because one's dedication is about oneself, it can shift gears from one object to the next. The object of my dedication is a constantly moving target and, frankly, it tends to move from whatever I used to think was best for myself to whatever I think is best for myself now. Perhaps it's a subtlety, but that's the way deception works. My dedication is a lot more about whatever it is that I am doing to demonstrate my commitment than it is about the thing or person to whom I am supposedly dedicated.

This is the problem with so much of what we call the Christian faith. It's really just trying to get people to amp up their dedication—you know, pray harder, fast faster, serve better, increase their tithes, and so it goes. The Christian faith is not about increasing one's dedication; it's about undivided devotion, abandoning oneself to God in love. Dedication is about self; devotion is about the other.

It's why Type #3 people are rare, but they embody the very core essence of the gospel. Can you believe what Jesus said in response to this woman's reckless act of devotion (pouring out a year's wages worth of perfume on his head)? Get this.

"And truly, I say to you, wherever the gospel is proclaimed in the whole world, what she has done will be told in memory of her."

I've said it before and I'll say it again. It makes me wonder if the corollary is also true—that wherever this story is not being told (and enacted) in memory of her if the gospel is even being preached.

Type #3 people are the goal. These are the kind of like-Jesus people the Holy Spirit longs to make. They should be the norm. So why do they tend to be the outliers?

The Prayer

Spirit of the living God, fall afresh on me.

The Questions

• What would it mean to trade in our passion to be more dedicated for a posture of abandoned devotion? What would that look like in your life?

75 The Key to Perceiving Revelation

MARK 14:12–16 NRSV | On the first day of Unleavened Bread, when the Passover lamb is sacrificed, his disciples said to him, "Where do you want us to go and make the preparations for you to eat the Passover?" So he sent two of his disciples, saying to them, "Go into the city, and a man carrying a jar of water will meet you; follow him, and wherever he enters, say to the owner of the house, 'The Teacher asks, Where is my guest room where I may eat the Passover with my disciples?' He will show you a large room upstairs, furnished and ready. Make preparations for us there." So the disciples set out and went to the city, and found everything as he had told them; and they prepared the Passover meal.

Consider This

And so we come to the fateful festival of the Passover. It's uncanny how everything has proceeded to this particular moment in history. The Lamb of God who takes away the sin of the world comes to celebrate the feast of the Passover Lamb. The destroyer of death comes to celebrate the remembrance of death's temporary reprieve. The blood of the lambs smeared over the door frames of Israel's homes for the ransom of their children will become the blood of Jesus poured out for the redemption of the children of God.

How could it have worked out so divinely perfect? Exactly.

The week of the death of Jesus holds layer upon layer of revelation. The challenging thing about revelation is that it must be revealed. The week of Jesus' passion can be grasped from a historical sense and still not perceived from the sense of revelation. Revelation requires eyes that see and ears that hear. To perceive divine revelation requires a pliable heart and a humble mind.

It's just so easy to come to chapter 14 of Mark's gospel and be blinded by the mentality that you've already been here and done this. We think we know what's going to happen, and in one sense we do. My hunch is we are barely scratching the surface of the depths of revelation contained in these final days in Jerusalem.

As we head into these final chapters of Mark's gospel, let's together pray for eyes to see and ears to hear and hearts to behold and minds to understand like we have never seen and heard and beheld and understood before. To see something is one thing, but to be gifted with insight is another thing entirely. There is a vast difference between looking *at* something and seeing *into* it. Perceiving revelation is about seeing into the nature of ultimate reality. It is the Holy Spirit's gift to the humble.

We will be well-served to remember Jesus' great prayer of reversal as we go forward: "At that time Jesus said, 'I praise you, Father, Lord of heaven and earth, because you have hidden these things from the wise and learned, and revealed them to little children'" (Matt. 11:25).

The Prayer

Spirit of the living God, fall afresh on me.

The Questions

- Where do you fall on the spectrum between the "wise and learned" or "little children"?

76 Getting in Touch with Our Inner Judas

MARK 14:17–21 | When evening came, Jesus arrived with the Twelve. While they were reclining at the table eating, he said, "Truly I tell you, one of you will betray me—one who is eating with me."

They were saddened, and one by one they said to him, "Surely you don't mean me?"

"It is one of the Twelve," he replied, "one who dips bread into the bowl with me. The Son of Man will go just as it is written about him. But woe to that man who betrays the Son of Man! It would be better for him if he had not been born."

Consider This

"Surely you don't mean me?"

We overestimate our saintliness and underestimate our sinfulness.

We overestimate our virtue and underestimate our vice.

We overestimate our strengths and underestimate our weaknesses.

We overestimate our "have-it-togetherness" and underestimate our brokenness.

So what's behind all this overestimation and underestimation? Pride, of course; a self-inflated vision of ourselves.

Pride clouds our vision of ourselves. No, it's worse than that. Pride blinds us to our own depravity.

So, what's the answer? How can we deal with that which we are unaware? We can cast ourselves on the mercy of our God. It brings to mind the ancient prayer known to the ages as "The Jesus Prayer." We've rehearsed it many times on the Daily Text.

"Lord Jesus Christ, Son of God, have mercy on me, a sinner."

This prayer contains the antidote to pride. It's not a prayer of shallow self-deprecation. It is a simple agreement with the truth about God and the truth about us. It's the kind of gut-level honesty that leads us to the place where instead of saying, "Surely you don't mean me," we humbly whisper, "There but for the grace of God go I."

This ancient moment before the Passover meal is a call to deep self-examination and repentance. As hard as it is to face, we must remain open to the possibility that it could always be "I." In fact, that's the only way to be sure it will not be.

The Prayer

Spirit of the living God, fall afresh on me.

The Questions

- Can you come to terms with your own capacity to betray Jesus?

Why I Never Understood the Lord's Supper Until . . .

MARK 14:22–26 ESV | And as they were eating, he took bread, and after blessing it broke it and gave it to them, and said, "Take; this is my body." And he took a cup, and when he had given thanks he gave it to them, and they all drank of it. And he said to them, "This is my blood of the a covenant, which is poured out for many. Truly, I say to you, I will not drink again of the fruit of the vine until that day when I drink it new in the kingdom of God."

And when they had sung a hymn, they went out to the Mount of Olives.

Consider This

"This is my body."
"This is my blood."

I must confess for much of my Christian life that I have not gotten the Lord's Supper. In fact, I still don't get it. I do, but I don't. In retrospect, I think I have missed it a lot precisely because I have tried to get it. My approach has been largely rational—trying to get my mind or thoughts around it to understand it so I could effectively receive it. Consequently, as I approached the altar to receive the sacrament, I focused on thinking the right thoughts and feeling the right feelings. I wanted to have thoughts and feelings of awe and gratitude and repentance and humility. And the problem with this way of thinking and feeling? Awe and gratitude and repentance and humility are not really thoughts and feelings, are they? They are deep dispositions of the heart.

It has never occurred to me until this very moment that when I am approaching the altar to receive the bread and the wine that I'm not entering into a religious ritual, I am celebrating a relationship. I am approaching a Person. I am approaching the person of Jesus Christ. He is not somehow contained in the gift of bread and wine. He *is* the gift. The physical reality of a person standing before me, giving me bread and wine while saying the very words of Jesus to me—it is as though I am approaching Jesus himself. The celebration of the Lord's Supper is not about approaching with the right thoughts and feelings, it's all about embracing Jesus himself.

No, I'm not talking about some kind of transubstantiation where the bread and the wine actually change their molecular properties to become the physical body and blood of Jesus. I do not want to denigrate that doctrine, as large parts of the church hold it dear. I just don't believe that is what this is all about.

This is more like a type of transfiguration—the transfiguration of a moment in which all of history seems to become suspended and we find ourselves in that Upper Room hearing Jesus himself say: "This is my body . . . this is my blood . . . for *you*." I am hearing this from Jesus himself. I am receiving the elements from Jesus himself. I am standing before the person of Jesus himself. He is present in the whole of it all, in the mystery of that encounter where we remember a historical event in a way that transcends history; in a way that brings it right into the moment of Holy Communion. Communion is not something we receive; it's a relationship we enter into and celebrate.

At its core essence, this is what I understand to be happening in this mystery. "This is my body," and "This is my blood," can be brought down to three very primal words: me for you. Jesus says to you and me personally and you and me in community, "me for you" in the sense of "God made him who had no sin to be sin for us, so that in him we might become the righteousness of God" (2 Cor. 5:21). It's "me for you" in the sense of, "If God is for us, who can be against us?" (Rom. 8:31). It's "me for you" in the sense of, "I have been crucified with Christ and I no longer live, but Christ lives in me. The life I now live in the body, I live by faith in the Son of God, who loved me and gave himself for me" (Gal. 2:20). It's "me for you" in the sense of "Abide in me as I abide in you. Just as the branch cannot bear fruit by itself unless it abides in the vine, neither can you unless you abide in me" (John 15:4 NRSV). It's "me for you" in the sense of the complete and total exchange of his wholeness for our brokenness and his fullness for our emptiness.

Here's the beauty of it all. What he most longs to receive from us in Holy Communion is to hear our wholehearted response of, "me for you," right back to him.

And here's the glory of it all. The truest sign of our entering into Holy Communion with Jesus is revealed and celebrated every time we approach another human being and welcome the Holy Spirit to demonstrate to them, through us, those same words, "me for you."

The Prayer

Spirit of the living God, fall afresh on me.

The Questions

- How are you understanding and approaching the Lord's Supper? Is it an essential part of your life or is it more of an occasional, optional thing?

On the Difference between Faith and Optimism

78

MARK 14:27–31 NRSV | And Jesus said to them, "You will all become deserters; for it is written,

'I will strike the shepherd,
  and the sheep will be scattered.'

But after I am raised up, I will go before you to Galilee." Peter said to him, "Even though all become deserters, I will not." Jesus said to him, "Truly I tell you, this day, this very night, before the cock crows twice, you will deny me three times." But he said vehemently, "Even though I must die with you, I will not deny you." And all of them said the same.

Consider This

Positive thinking is overrated. It anchors itself in self-confidence. It makes bold declarations and promises as though projecting the outcome will make it so. Positive thinking or optimism is powerful because it roots itself so deeply in the pride form of the human psyche. Let me be clear, though. Positive thinking is not all bad, it's just overrated. The critical distinction we must constantly make is the difference between positive thinking and faith.

Positive thinking ties our faith to some preconceived and hoped for outcome. Faith, on the other hand, does not seek a particular outcome, but rather anchors all hope in God alone and the surety of his promises.

I want you to notice how this dynamic distinction between faith and optimism work out in today's text. Jesus makes two simple declarations: 1. *"You will all become deserters."* 2. *"But after I am raised up, I will go before you to Galilee."*

Go back and scan the text again. Note how #1 gets all the action and #2 doesn't even get honorable mention in the conversation. Each and every one of the disciples confused positive thinking for faith, and, as a result, in the face of

Jesus' challenge, they doubled down on their self-confidence and completely missed his promise. Jesus gives them the promise of an ultimate future. They put their confidence in themselves and their own projected outcome. How did they completely miss what he said? My theory: they could not accept the truth he told them about themselves. He told them they would not be able to endure what was about to happen; that their frailty would lead to their failure. He essentially told them their loyalty would not last because it was built on the lie they told themselves—that they could do it—rather than on the truth of the resurrection promise.

Permit me what may be a pastoral digression and yet I hope a faithful application.

What about us? So you have cancer or debilitating depression or a crumbling marriage or an impending bankruptcy or a wayward son or daughter. Let go of your hopeful projection of a certain outcome. Accept, no, embrace the brokenness of your situation and your powerlessness to hold it all together. Release your self-confidence so that faith can arise in the God and Father of our risen Lord, Jesus Christ. The greatest gift in the darkness of our struggles will be our dying to the false god of our particular expectations we have for resolution and releasing our struggle to the God who is raised from the dead who goes ahead of us.

A powerful faith story from the life of Abraham seems apropos. En route to do the unthinkable—to sacrifice his only son, Isaac, as a burnt offering in response to the calling of God we get this exchange:

On the third day Abraham looked up and saw the place in the distance. He said to his servants, "Stay here with the donkey while I and the boy go over there. We will worship and then we will come back to you."

Abraham took the wood for the burnt offering and placed it on his son Isaac, and he himself carried the fire and the knife. As the two of them went on together, Isaac spoke up and said to his father Abraham, "Father?"

"Yes, my son?" Abraham replied.

"The fire and wood are here," Isaac said, "but where is the lamb for the burnt offering?"

Abraham answered, "God himself will provide the lamb for the burnt offering, my son." And the two of them went on together. (Gen. 22:4–8)

Did you see Abraham's faith? He did not know how, but he knew God.

Now observe how the writer of Hebrews sums this up:

By faith Abraham, when God tested him, offered Isaac as a sacrifice. He who had embraced the promises was about to sacrifice his one and only son, even though God had said to him, "It is through Isaac that your offspring will be reckoned." Abraham reasoned that God could even raise the dead, and so in a manner of speaking he did receive Isaac back from death. (Heb. 11:17–19)

Real faith clings to Jesus alone and surrenders to his resolution which always involves resurrection, sooner or later.

I want to suggest a way of faith in the face of the most difficult places in life—both yours and of those you love. Pray something like this—over and over: "Resurrection, Jesus. I don't know how, but I pray resurrection, Jesus."

The Prayer

Spirit of the living God, fall afresh on me.

The Questions

- What if our faith is actually only an optimistic clinging to our hope in a particular outcome we have in mind? What if real faith can only arise in the wake of the death of our optimism and positive thinking?
- How do you relate to the distinction between optimism and faith?

Why There's No Place for "If" in Prayer

79

MARK 14:32–36 | They went to a place called Gethsemane, and Jesus said to his disciples, "Sit here while I pray." He took Peter, James and John along with him, and he began to be deeply distressed and troubled. "My soul is overwhelmed with sorrow to the point of death," he said to them. "Stay here and keep watch."

Going a little farther, he fell to the ground and prayed that if possible the hour might pass from him. "Abba, Father," he said, "everything is possible for you. Take this cup from me. Yet not what I will, but what you will."

Consider This

The world went wrong in a garden, the garden of Eden. Is it any surprise the world would be turned around in a garden, the garden of Gethsemane. The cross was unutterably painful and shameful, but the real suffering went down that night under the ancient olive trees of Gethsemane (a.k.a. "The Olive Press").

We will get to the disciples tomorrow, but for today, we need to fix our study on Jesus. Get back in touch with the scene. The Last Supper just happened. Jesus and the disciples left the city, crossed the Kidron Valley, and ascended back up the hillside known as the Mount of Olives. This garden was a familiar spot for them. Jesus had his go-to places of meeting with the Father. This was his Jerusalem location. (As a sidebar, have you found some "go-to" places for prayer? If not, ask Jesus to lead you to such places.)

As we make our way into the garden, we see a group of eight men sitting under the trees together. Going a little further we see a group of three men who look to be asleep. Walking about a stone's throw further we find the Son of God. He's on his knees, face to the ground. He is weeping. No, he is crying—the kind of crying where you can't stop, where your guts heave uncontrollably.

"My soul is overwhelmed with sorrow to the point of death," he confided to the three just moments earlier.

If we listen—no, if we have ears to hear—we can hear him praying. At this moment in history, in this particular place, we behold the second person of the Trinity speaking with the first person of the Trinity in the bonded fellowship of the third person of the Trinity. Astonishingly enough, we actually know at least part of his prayer:

"Abba, Father," he said, "everything is possible for you. Take this cup from me. Yet not what I will but what you will."

Recall when we talked about faith not being in some particular outcome but in God alone, come what may. Well, this is that. So, what can we learn here?

"Abba, Father." No one in their right mind called God, "Abba." This would have been out of place in the Jewish understanding of God; kind of like it feels out of place when people refer to God as "Daddy" in their prayers today. Yet "Daddy" is precisely what Jesus was saying, and whether we had this kind of earthly parent or not, Jesus shows us, as a matter of fact, this is who God is to us. (Healing does not come by running away from the brokenness inflicted upon one from a parental relationship but by the long arduous process of working through it—as painful as it can be—and for clarity's sake, I'm not speaking of a happily-ever-after reconciliation but rather forgiveness.)

"Everything is possible for you." This is faith; not in a particular outcome but in any possible outcome. We remind God of this not for his sake but for our sake. When Sarah laughed at the news of her impending pregnancy in her old age, the angel said, "Is anything too hard for the

Lord?" (Gen. 18:14). When the Lord asked the prophet Jeremiah to purchase land on the eve of the Babylonian exile whose value within days would be less than zero, God responded, "I am the Lord, the God of all mankind. Is anything too hard for me?" (Jer. 32:27). When the angel Gabriel visited the Virgin Mary with the news of her impending pregnancy with the Son of God, he said to her, "For nothing will be impossible with God" (Luke 1:37 NRSV). When everything is possible for God, we need not worry about anything being impossible.

Because everything is possible with God, we should feel the bold freedom to ask God for anything. While the prayer, "Take this cup from me," may not always be in the cards, it is always in order to ask. Jesus clearly offers a prayer to Abba that is not in the will of God. Though Jesus was always fully human, this was perhaps his most human moment—crying out in agony to God with a prayer that will not be granted.

"*Yet not what I will but what you will.*" It always bothers me when people preface their prayers by saying, "If it's your will." You know what I'm talking about. "And, God, if it's your will, would you heal this disease?" Note: Jesus did not pray, "If it's your will, let this cup pass me by." He prayed, "*Take this cup from me.*" Huge difference here. Only after the clear imperative did he offer yet another imperative—"*Yet not what I will but what you will.*" This is not a subtle distinction; it's massive. If you ever want to pray for me, please never use the word "if." Just go for it.

Do you know the simple translation for "Yet not what I will but what you will"? Three words, *I trust you.*

And it's a thousand miles of maturity from "Take this cup from me," to "Not my will but what you will."

Me? I'm somewhere in between; making progress but not there yet. How about you?

The Prayer

Spirit of the living God, fall afresh on me.

The Questions

· What keeps you back from a whole-hearted "Not my will but what you will" kind of prayer, especially in the difficult places in life?

The Lord Helps Those Who Help Themselves . . . Sort Of

80

MARK 14:37–42 ESV | And he came and found them sleeping, and he said to Peter, "Simon, are you asleep? Could you not watch one hour? Watch and pray that you may not enter into temptation. The spirit indeed is willing, but the flesh is weak." And again he went away and prayed, saying the same words. And again he came and found them sleeping, for their eyes were very heavy, and they did not know what to answer him. And he came the third time and said to them, "Are you still sleeping and taking your rest? It is enough; the hour has come. The Son of Man is betrayed into the hands of sinners. Rise, let us be going; see, my betrayer is at hand."

Consider This

Surely you've heard it said before, "Well, the Bible does say, 'The Lord helps those who help themselves.'" The punchline, of course, is the Bible does not actually say this. As I have reflected on today's text, however, I think it just may.

For most of my years of reading this text I looked at it as though Jesus was trying to get these three disciples to support and pray for him in his hour of need. It seems logical enough. Why else would he have pulled them out of the group?

Then I saw the text perhaps more clearly.

"Watch and pray that you may not enter into temptation."

Jesus was not asking them to pray for him but to pray for themselves. In his hour of greatest struggle, Jesus was concerned for these three. And why these three? Remember James and John's request to sit at his right and left hand in his kingdom? Remember Peter's bold declaration that he would go to the death with Jesus? Jesus knew they were in grave danger.

Why did he keep coming back to them, a second and third time? It had to be because he was concerned about them. Jesus was doing everything possible to warn them and to protect them and, even at this eleventh hour, to instruct and equip them.

"The spirit indeed is willing, but the flesh is weak."

It's like he was saying to them, "There's only so much I can do with you, but I can't do it for you. I can help you but you have to be willing to help yourselves here." The spirit is willing, but it is up to us to take hold of the willingness of the spirit. The flesh is weak, but it is up to us to humbly confess our frailty and slay our pride so that our willingness can embrace the spirit's willingness. The weakness of the flesh is shrouded in the delusion of self-made strength.

There are so many times in life where we completely miss the spirit's willingness because we think we have what it takes to get the job done. We become the kind of people who proudly say, "The Lord helps those who help themselves," by which we mean, "I'm not waiting around on the Lord. I've got this." These are precisely the kind of people the Lord can't help.

This is where the kingdom of God gets incredibly counter-intuitive. The only way we help ourselves in the kingdom of God is reaching the end of ourselves where we can honestly say, "I can't help myself." Jesus put it this way, "Blessed are the poor in spirit, for theirs is the kingdom of heaven" (Matt. 5:3). Track carefully with me here. Our willfulness parades as our strength, but it is actually our greatest weakness. Until we can cast aside the weakness of our willfulness, we will never be able to take hold of the strength of the spirit's willingness.

This is why, as they say, "Pride goes before a fall." This was the fate of Peter, James, and John, who because they were so strong in themselves they never had any idea they needed the strength of the spirit—until it was too late.

So the Lord does help those who help themselves . . . sort of. The Lord mightily helps those who come to the end of themselves and realize they cannot help themselves, which turns out to be the most ironic twist of them all. Only those who embrace their helplessness (i.e., the poor in spirit) qualify for the kingdom.

It's so easy to spot this kind of glaring weakness (the pride of one's willfulness and strength) in others, yet so hard to see it in ourselves.

The Prayer

Spirit of the living God, fall afresh on me.

The Questions

- Why is it easy to spot pride in others yet hard to see it in ourselves?

- Is there anyone you have given permission to point out this type of weakness in your life?

81 The Wound That Never Heals

MARK 14:43–52 NRSV | Immediately, while he was still speaking, Judas, one of the twelve, arrived; and with him there was a crowd with swords and clubs, from the chief priests, the scribes, and the elders. Now the betrayer had given them a sign, saying, "The one I will kiss is the man; arrest him and lead him away under guard." So when he came, he went up to him at once and said, "Rabbi!" and kissed him. Then they laid hands on him and arrested him. But one of those who stood near drew his sword and struck the slave of the high priest, cutting off his ear. Then Jesus said to them, "Have you come out with swords and clubs to arrest me as though I were a bandit? Day after day I was with you in the temple teaching, and you did not arrest me. But let the scriptures be fulfilled." All of them deserted him and fled.

A certain young man was following him, wearing nothing but a linen cloth. They caught hold of him, but he left the linen cloth and ran off naked.

Consider This

Judas betrayed him and everyone else deserted him. 11 + 1 = 12.

But there was a thirteenth.

A certain young man was following him, wearing nothing but a linen cloth. They caught hold of him, but he left the linen cloth and ran off naked.

Tradition tells it was Mark from the Gospel of Mark.

Back to the betrayal. Betrayal may be the worst offense a person could possibly commit. Why? Because it takes a friend to betray you. It's why betrayal is something you can get past, but never get over. It is a mortal wound.

The Prayer

Spirit of the living God, fall afresh on me.

The Questions

- Have you ever experienced betrayal? Have you ever betrayed?

82 The Reason behind Most Discipleship Failures

MARK 14:53–59 | They took Jesus to the high priest, and all the chief priests, the elders and the teachers of the law came together. Peter followed him at a distance, right into the courtyard of the high priest. There he sat with the guards and warmed himself at the fire.

The chief priests and the whole Sanhedrin were looking for evidence against Jesus so that they could put him to death, but they did not find any. Many testified falsely against him, but their statements did not agree.

Then some stood up and gave this false testimony against him: "We heard him say, 'I will destroy this temple made with human hands and in three days will build another, not made with hands.'" Yet even then their testimony did not agree.

Consider This

I would like to make an observation about today's text, which I think holds the key to most discipleship failures. It's right there in verse 54.

Peter followed him at a distance . . .

Just a few verses back we saw Peter run for the hills with the rest of the disciples. Apparently, somewhere between fourth and fifth gear, he remembered the loyalty pledge he made to Jesus a few short hours earlier.

Just as his oath was fueled by his best intentions and the strength of his ego, so was his half-hearted return from his terrified retreat. There's a way of following Jesus from the strength of the Holy Spirit, and there's a way of following Jesus from the strength of the human spirit. The interesting irony of the latter is the way these Peter types have all the appearances of being all in, when the truth of the matter is they are really only following him from a distance.

I have a friend Lauren, who categorizes people into two basic groups: the people who have dealt and the people who have not dealt. What does she mean by this? I'm glad you asked. She's talking about people who are stuck somewhere between forgiveness and freedom. Many, if not most, people stop growing when they receive the first gift of salvation— the forgiveness of their sins. For many reasons, all of which will be profoundly unsatisfying in the end, they fail to press on from the gift of forgiveness to greater gifts of freedom in Christ and the fullness of the Holy Spirit. The result is that they tend to follow Jesus at a distance. As we discussed the other day, they put on a show of commitment, which masks their deficit of devotion.

And that's the crazy thing about it. No one would have ever accused Peter of following at a distance. He looked to the world like disciple 1A.

The truth? Following from a distance isn't really following at all. When we follow from a distance we trade in our discipleship for a place in the crowd. We will see soon how distance fosters denial, which is the recipe for a discipleship failure.

So who follows Jesus up close? It's the ones who have dealt. It's the people who have broken through the barrier of their brokenness only to discover their blessedness. They are the poor in spirit, those who mourn, the meek, the ones who hunger and thirst for righteousness beyond religiosity, who crave mercy, whose hearts radiate the pure love of God, who breathe peace everywhere they go, and who receive the persecution of enemies as a badge of honor.

Those who follow Jesus up close have come to the realization that it's the only way they can make it.

All of this has me asking myself, *Where am I in the mix?* It probably looks like I'm following pretty closely, which is what scares me. How about you?

The Prayer

Spirit of the living God, fall afresh on me.

The Questions

- Where are you in the mix?

How Faith Is like a "Get out of Jail Free" Card, and How It's Not

MARK 14:60–65 ESV | And the high priest stood up in the midst and asked Jesus, "Have you no answer to make? What is it that these men testify against you?" But he remained silent and made no answer. Again the high priest asked him, "Are you the Christ, the Son of the Blessed?" And Jesus said, "I am, and you will see the Son of Man seated at the right hand of Power, and coming with the clouds of heaven." And the high priest tore his garments and said, "What further witnesses do we need? You have heard his blasphemy. What is your decision?" And they all condemned him as deserving death. And some began to spit on him and to cover his face and to strike him, saying to him, "Prophesy!" And the guards received him with blows.

Consider This

Mark, throughout his Gospel account, carefully unfolds two different but hopelessly intertwining storylines. On many occasions, he tells us the story from the perspective of Jesus, after which he will tell us the story from the perspective of the people. Now, the perspective of the people is actually made up of the multiple perspectives of the religious leadership, the common people, and Jesus' disciples. Interestingly enough, while the perspectives of the people differed in many ways, they were all basically the same. The people, from the Sanhedrin to the Twelve, saw Jesus through the lenses of first-century messianic expectations. They were looking for a political leader who would affect a revolutionary deliverance from the immediate oppression of Rome.

Back in Mark 8 we get this exchange between Jesus and his disciples.

> "But what about you?" he asked. "Who do you say I am?"
>
> Peter answered, "You are the Messiah."
>
> Jesus warned them not to tell anyone about him.
>
> He then began to teach them that the Son of Man must suffer many things and be rejected by the elders, the chief priests and the teachers of the law, and that he must be killed and after three days rise again. He spoke plainly about this, and Peter took him aside and began to rebuke him. (Mark 8:29–32)

In today's text we get this exchange between Jesus and the religious establishment:

Again the high priest asked him, "Are you the Christ, the Son of the Blessed?" And Jesus said, "I am, and you will see the Son of Man seated at the right hand of Power, and coming with the clouds of heaven."

Look at the interplay here. Peter says, "You are the Messiah," while the high priest says, "Are you the Messiah?" Peter and Caiaphas were talking about the same thing—their own concept of who the Messiah would be and what he would do. To them, Messiah meant god-like power and authority, but it did not mean God. This brings us to the profound ironic twist of today's text. Here is God, in disguise, arrested and bound and on trial by the leaders of his chosen people for his claim to messianic status and he plays the ultimate God card. It is as though he were saying, "You think I am claiming to be the Messiah, and I am, but what you really need to know here is you aren't dealing with a Messiah who is a threat to your power as you imagine it or as a solution to your problems as my disciples conceive of it. The eternal Judge of heaven and earth stands before you and is bringing a deliverance that will make your petty political problems seem like a playground scuffle over a game of marbles. You are looking for the defeat of your political enemies. I have come to defeat the supreme enemy of the powers of evil. And one more thing. Your rejection of me and my crucifixion will turn out to be my resurrection from the dead and the eternal redemption of all who will believe in my name, which could even include you."

That's my take on Jesus' trial before the Sanhedrin this time through. But here's where I wrestle with it and perhaps you do too. So what difference does all this make for me and my challenges and problems today and tomorrow and the next day? Like you, I'm facing some pretty hard things from which I need immediate deliverance. What does all this biblical analysis have to do with anything that matters right now?

I think that's my point. I need Jesus to be and do certain things for me right now. If he does them, I will be ecstatic. If he does not, I will be devastated. This has the perhaps unintended effect of putting him on trial today. Certainly Jesus can solve your and my problems, but this is not who he is and what faith is all about. He is not our domestic Messiah. He is the God of heaven and earth who has defeated sin and death. We may get a reprieve from our cancer, but it will be back—in one form or another. The victory of God is that cancer does not ultimately win. And because cancer will lose, we have a completely different way of dealing with it now. When you know you are going to win, you play the game differently.

Even better, when you know the God of heaven and earth is closer than your breath, you play with joyful boldness—come what may. (It's kind of like in Monopoly when you get the "Get out of Jail Free" card.)

These two stories, told from the perspective of Jesus and understood from our own limited perspective, continue to unfold in an intertwining fashion right up to the present moment. In the short term, we are going to win some big ones and we will lose some really hard ones. Faith literally means living right now—win, lose, or draw—from the eternal perspective of Jesus. This does not mean deferring everything to the eternal hereafter—it means having the audacity to actually live in the eternal hereafter, right here and now.

The Prayer

Spirit of the living God, fall afresh on me.

The Questions

- On a scale from 1–10, with 10 meaning "I am winning, even though it looks like I am losing," and 1 meaning, "I'm losing the battle and I've lost sight of who I thought God was," where do you fall?

The Journey of Peter and the Journey of Us

84

MARK 14:66–72 NRSV | While Peter was below in the courtyard, one of the servant-girls of the high priest came by. When she saw Peter warming himself, she stared at him and said, "You also were with Jesus, the man from Nazareth." But he denied it, saying, "I do not know or understand what you are talking about." And he went out into the forecourt. Then the cock crowed. And the servant-girl, on seeing him, began again to say to the bystanders, "This man is one of them." But again he denied it. Then after a little while the bystanders again said to Peter, "Certainly you are one of them; for you are a Galilean." But he began to curse, and he swore an oath, "I do not know this man you are talking about." At that moment the cock crowed for the second time. Then Peter remembered that Jesus had said to him, "Before the cock crows twice, you will deny me three times." And he broke down and wept.

Consider This

Do you remember those early days soon after Peter first met Jesus? They were cleaning their nets after a night of catching nothing when Jesus approached and told them to throw their nets out into the deep waters. It led to a miraculous catch of fish. Luke records Peter's response as, "When Simon Peter saw this, he fell at Jesus' knees and said, 'Go away from me, Lord; I am a sinful man!'" (Luke 5:8).

Do you remember that day when Peter made his famous confession of Christ at Caesarea Philippi? Matthew has it this way: "'But what about you?' he asked. 'Who do you say I am?' Simon Peter answered, 'You are the Messiah, the Son of the living God'" (Matt. 16:15–16).

Then there was that time just a few days ago at the Last Supper when Jesus told his disciples they would all abandon him:

> Peter replied, "Even if all fall away on account of you, I never will."
>
> "Truly I tell you," Jesus answered, "this very night, before the rooster crows, you will disown me three times."
>
> But Peter declared, "Even if I have to die with you, I will never disown you." And all the other disciples said the same. (Matt. 26:33–35)

It brings us to today's text with Peter being confronted in the courtyard of the home of the chief priest.

Denial #1: *"I do not know or understand what you are talking about."*

Denial #2: *And the servant-girl, on seeing him, began again to say to the bystanders, "This man is one of them." But again he denied it.*

Denial #3: *But he began to curse, and he swore an oath, "I do not know this man you are talking about."*

There's a progression of discipleship here in the life of Peter. I think it's common to most pathways of discipleship.

It began with his early encounters of Jesus and his profound experience of humility. It's interesting though how being humbled doesn't always translate into long-term humility. We can follow Jesus for years, thinking we are his ultimate insiders, while our veiled pride actually keeps us following at a distance. Somewhere along the way, by the mercy of God, we hit a wall. It might be a testing of our mettle where we come up lacking. It may be a midlife crisis or, even better, a midlife awakening. Whatever it is, we are brought face-to-face with an emptiness we once mistook for fullness.

Betsy, a member of our Daily Text community, corresponds with me regularly to share thoughts and insights. Just the other day she shared a story of a trip to Israel and visiting three classic statutes of Peter. Here's Betsy (with her permission) in her own words:

> The first is outside Capernaum and shows Peter as "The Rock" who has it all together—at that point in time that was who I used to be. The second is in Jerusalem after Jesus' arrest when he "followed at a distance." I could very much relate to the confusion shown in Peter's face of, "I thought I had this all figured out, but yet nothing is making sense. This is not how it was supposed to play out. I don't know what to do. I don't know what to believe." The third statue commemorates when Peter met Jesus on the shores of the Sea of Galilee after the resurrection. I instinctively knew that was where I needed to get to. I found it interesting that

most of us in the group felt like our visit to the site of the third statue was way too short. There was a need to stay longer and wait.

There's nothing like honest discipleship. Betsy shows us what the second half of the gospel journey looks like. It presses past an easy self-confidence parading as faith. It leads to disorientation and through brokenness and onward to surrender and restoration. I wonder where you find your-self on the journey today. What holds you back?

The Prayer

Spirit of the living God, fall afresh on me.

The Questions

- Sometimes all it takes is simple honesty with ourselves before God to get unstuck. What might that look like for you today?

85 Why Are You So Defensive?

MARK 15:1–5 | Very early in the morning, the chief priests, with the elders, the teachers of the law and the whole Sanhedrin, made their plans. So they bound Jesus, led him away and handed him over to Pilate.

"Are you the king of the Jews?" asked Pilate.

"You have said so," Jesus replied.

The chief priests accused him of many things. So again Pilate asked him, "Aren't you going to answer? See how many things they are accusing you of."

But Jesus still made no reply, and Pilate was amazed.

Consider This

Given a chance, people who are accused of something will defend themselves and typically refocus the blame on someone else. Human beings are instinctively defensive creatures. One might say, it's in our genes. Remember this from the early days?

> And he said, "Who told you that you were naked? Have you eaten from the tree that I commanded you not to eat from?"
>
> The man said, "The woman you put here with me— she gave me some fruit from the tree, and I ate it."
>
> Then the LORD God said to the woman, "What is this you have done?"
>
> The woman said, "The serpent deceived me, and I ate." (Gen. 3:11–13)

From the youngest children to the oldest adults, we hate being accused of something we did not do or for which we are not responsible. It violates our rights and sense of justice.

Not Jesus.

The chief priests accused him of many things. So again Pilate asked him, "Aren't you going to answer? See how many things they are accusing you of."

But Jesus still made no reply, and Pilate was amazed.

Jesus submitted to the jurisdiction of Pilate and his court, but he chose not to dignify it with a defense. Jesus stood in Pilate's chambers, but for him another court was in session. As Peter tells us in his letter: "When they hurled their insults at him, he did not retaliate; when he suffered, he made no threats. Instead, he entrusted himself to him who judges justly" (1 Peter 2:23).

There it is. "Instead, he entrusted himself to him who judges justly."

Many believe Peter was Mark's primary source in the writing of the Gospel account. This particular Gospel would find major traction in Rome with the Christians there who suffered under immense persecution. This account of Jesus' passion served as a literal handbook for the way they would deal with the same kinds of situations. They would not defend themselves, but instead would entrust themselves to him who judges justly.

Though my everyday life seems a thousand miles away from being put on trial for following Jesus, I do find a hundred daily scenarios in which I feel the need to defend myself. Whether it be big issues at work or trivial disputes around the house, I find that I need to be right and this need leads me to defend my position. This need to be right goes by another name: self-righteousness, and the need to defend myself is also known as "self-vindication." Why do we do this? I think it's because our own sense of security is primarily rooted in ourselves and our ability to protect ourselves. We mostly entrust ourselves to ourselves, and that's our biggest problem.

What if we could live from a far deeper source of security? What if we could "entrust ourselves to him who judges justly"? What if we could really live in the constancy of a higher court, entrusting ourselves to God instead of constantly serving as our own lawyer?

I've got a challenge for us, just for today. Could you and I make it through an entire day without defending ourselves or becoming defensive in the face of some offense? While this is a far cry from being on trial for our faith, the same deep impulses are at work. If we can't entrust ourselves to him who judges justly in the smallest things, how on earth will we do it in the big things?

I believe this could be one of the most critical areas of maturity for our discipleship. I know I struggle with it. I know you do too.

The Prayer

Spirit of the living God, fall afresh on me.

The Questions

- Are you a defensive person who feels the need to justify yourself or be right? What might it look like to entrust yourself to the protection of God more than needing to vindicate yourself?

86 Why It's All Your Fault

MARK 15:6–15 ESV | Now at the feast he used to release for them one prisoner for whom they asked. And among the rebels in prison, who had committed murder in the insurrection, there was a man called Barabbas. And the crowd came up and began to ask Pilate to do as he usually did for them. And he answered them, saying, "Do you want me to release for you the King of the Jews?" For he perceived that it was out of envy that the chief priests had delivered him up. But the chief priests stirred up the crowd to have him release for them Barabbas instead. And Pilate again said to them, "Then what shall I do with the man you call the King of the Jews?" And they cried out again, "Crucify him." And Pilate said to them, "Why? What evil has he done?" But they shouted all the more, "Crucify him." So Pilate, wishing to satisfy the crowd, released for them Barabbas, and having scourged Jesus, he delivered him to be crucified.

Consider This

And Pilate again said to them, "Then what shall I do with the man you call the King of the Jews?" And they cried out again, "Crucify him." And Pilate said to them, "Why? What evil has he done?" But they shouted all the more, "Crucify him."

Crowds are insanely dangerous entities. In a crowd, no particular person holds power, yet together they hold a collective form of power bordering on absolute. Because no individual person holds power, no individual can be held responsible. This explains the danger of a crowd: extraordinary power without personal responsibility.

Isn't this what killed Jesus? Sure, we can blame the religious leaders, and we can blame Pilate. We can even blame Judas. What good will it do, though, to blame the crowd? This is precisely the way we escape personal responsibility. We delegate our guilt to the crowd where it can never be absolved because it will never be felt. The crowd never pleads guilty. This is how the gravest of injustices happen.

In fact, this is how the greatest injustice in history went down. The gospel of Jesus Christ is how the gravest injustice in the history of the world became the most gracious invitation for all eternity to come. The miracle of redemption happened because the blameless one took our blame. He was crucified by the collective crowd of the human race, all of us together. We don't stand in the shoes of the Sanhedrin. We can't play the role of Judas. While we may identify with Peter, we can't play his part either. We, the human race, find our voices in the voice of the crowd, in the cruelty of their collective cry, "Crucify him!"

Did you see what I did there: "in the cruelty of their collective cry?" Who is "their"? Exactly! "Their" is "them." And "they" are always someone other than me.

The crowd killed Jesus, but grace can't be received by a crowd. Grace can only be received by a person. That's what salvation by grace through faith means. It happens when I decide to step out of the crowd and take personal responsibility, not for my part of the crime, but for the whole thing—as though it were solely my fault. Only then do I finally realize the person who bore no responsibility for any of it actually took on total responsibility for all of it. Salvation by grace through faith means coming to the experiential ownership that I deserve all the blame, yet because of the finished work of Jesus' death and resurrection, I am now deemed blameless. It was my fault, but I am deemed faultless. I simply cannot bear that responsibility; neither can I absolve myself of it. Only God can.

It astonishes me even to write it, much less speak it aloud. I only need believe it. Only that will make me the kind of person God had in mind when he first imagined me. There is no better news than this. This, my friends, is the gospel.

The Prayer
Spirit of the living God, fall afresh on me.

The Questions
- Does it seem like an injustice for you to accept total responsibility for the death of Jesus? If so, why?

Why You Should Not Be Ashamed of Yourself

87

MARK 15:16–20 NRSV | Then the soldiers led him into the courtyard of the palace (that is, the governor's headquarters); and they called together the whole cohort. And they clothed him in a purple cloak; and after twisting some thorns into a crown, they put it on him. And they began saluting him, "Hail, King of the Jews!" They struck his head with a reed, spat upon him, and knelt down in homage to him. After mocking him, they stripped him of the purple cloak and put his own clothes on him. Then they led him out to crucify him.

Consider This

Why is the suffering of Jesus recorded in such great detail?

Why didn't the Holy Spirit instruct Mark to cut to the chase and say something like, "The soldiers mocked Jesus and then they led him out to crucify him."

Then the soldiers led him into the courtyard of the palace (that is, the governor's headquarters); and they called together the whole cohort. And they clothed him in a purple cloak; and after twisting some thorns into a crown, they put it on him. And they began saluting him, "Hail, King of the Jews!" They struck his head with a reed, spat upon him, and knelt down in homage to him. After mocking him, they stripped him of the purple cloak and put his own clothes on him. Then they led him out to crucify him.

I think the Spirit wanted us to see the depths to which Jesus not only took on our guilt but bore our shame. To experience guilt means coming to the realization that we have done a bad thing that has caused injury to another. The proper response to guilt is confession and repentance. Shame is guilt gone wrong. Where guilt confesses to another, "I have done bad," shame turns in on oneself and claims, "I am bad." To shame someone is not to condemn their behavior but to condemn their personhood. Shame short-circuits confession and precludes repentance because it traps us within a prison of our own making. Just as we cannot absolve our own guilt, we cannot escape our own shame. Guilt is our fundamental problem. Shame is our fundamental condition. We can only be saved from such a problem and delivered from such a condition. Our greatest need is for salvation and deliverance, a savior and a deliverer.

Herein lies the glory of the cross. Crucifixion is the public proclamation of guilt wrapped up in the permanent exposure of shame. Crucifixion says not only have you done evil but that you are worthless. Here's the gospel: Jesus took the most horrific sign of guilt and shame and transformed it into the most beautiful sign of forgiveness and honor. This is why we can declare, "For I am not ashamed of the gospel, because it is the power of God that brings salvation to everyone who believes: first to the Jew, then to the Gentile" (Rom. 1:16). It's why we can say, "For the message of the cross is foolishness to those who are perishing, but to us who are being saved it is the power of God" (1 Cor. 1:18).

Because of Jesus' death and resurrection, the message of the cross is forgiveness from our guilt and the deliverance from our shame.

> Therefore, since we are surrounded by such a great cloud of witnesses, let us throw off everything that hinders and the sin that so easily entangles. And let us run with perseverance the race marked out for us, fixing our eyes on Jesus, the pioneer and perfecter of faith. For the joy set before him he endured the cross, scorning its shame, and sat down at the right hand of the throne of God. (Heb. 12:1–2)

The Prayer
Spirit of the living God, fall afresh on me.

The Questions
- Can you see the difference between guilt and shame and how the latter masquerades as the former?
- Can you behold Jesus in today's text taking on your shame? What would it mean to let him have it?

The Glorious Imposition of the Cross

88

MARK 15:21–26 | A certain man from Cyrene, Simon, the father of Alexander and Rufus, was passing by on his way in from the country, and they forced him to carry the cross. They brought Jesus to the place called Golgotha (which means "the place of the skull"). Then they offered him wine mixed with myrrh, but he did not take it. And they crucified him. Dividing up his clothes, they cast lots to see what each would get.

It was nine in the morning when they crucified him. The written notice of the charge against him read: THE KING OF THE JEWS.

Consider This

Here was a man minding his own business, when he comes upon the unfortunate death march of a few common criminals. Rome always made a public spectacle of crucifixions as a way of keeping the citizenry in check signaling their imperial power.

He must have looked strong compared with others in the crowd. He probably had no idea who Jesus was. At least we know he didn't volunteer to help. The text is careful to tell us "they forced him to carry the cross." I suspect his clothes were stained with the blood of Jesus by the time he arrived at Golgotha. We don't know where he was going that day. His day was another ordinary day, just like yesterday or today was for us. This event was not on his calendar. It was a violent interruption of his agenda. Imagine being forced to provide aid to a publicly condemned criminal. My money says Simon had no idea what was going on that day.

I imagine his family back home, waiting for him after he missed dinner and wondering what happened. This would not have been a great story he told them. This was humiliating and shameful. He had been treated as a common criminal by the authorities. He was forced to stand in the stead of a convicted criminal. I wonder how Alexander and Rufus handled it when the word got around to their friends about their father being abused by the authorities. They probably felt shame by association.

It's curious to me why Mark would tell us the names of the sons of Simon from Cyrene when he allows the woman at Bethany to remain anonymous. This woman whose story Jesus said would accompany his all over the world remains unnamed while we know the names of the sons of the man forced to carry the cross of Jesus. I'll bet they were ashamed of their father and what he had been forced to do.

Something tells me Rufus and Alexander became powerful heralds of the gospel. Something tells me their scornful shame transformed into significant status three days later when reports swept across the land that this so-called criminal, Jesus of Nazareth, had risen from the dead. Imagine their friends pointing across the way at Rufus and Alexander, whispering to another, "Their dad was the one who carried the cross of the man who was raised from the dead."

Today, two thousand years later, we are still telling the story of Simon of Cyrene. He is easily one of the most famous people in the history of the world. Compare the number of people who have heard Simon's story to those who have heard the name of (choose your own celebrity). Everywhere the Word of God goes, the story of Simon of Cyrene gets told, and Rufus and Alexander get honorable mention. It's the story of the glorious imposition of the cross.

There's a subtle and ironic illustration of the great parable of the final judgment tucked in the folds of this story. You remember the one where Jesus said, "As you have done it unto the least of these my brethren, you have done it unto me" (see Matthew 25:40)? Isn't that precisely and quite literally Simon's story? In carrying the cross of a condemned criminal, he bore the burden of God.

The truth is, it's our story too. What if every chance we have to carry the cross and bear the burden of one of the least and the last and the lost in this world we are actually carrying the cross of Jesus? It's worth considering. It might even be a good thing if somewhere along the way it were somehow imposed on us. I'm trying to be open to that. How about you? Imagine how it changed the life and destiny of Rufus and Alexander. Imagine how it might gloriously change the life and destiny of our families. Talk about a legacy!

I can't help but think that Rufus is that same Rufus Paul sent greetings to in his letter to the Romans when he wrote, "Greet Rufus, chosen in the Lord, and his mother, who has been a mother to me, too" (Rom. 16:13).

The Prayer

Spirit of the living God, fall afresh on me.

The Questions

- Can you recall a time when carrying the cross of another was imposed on you—some hardship or struggle of someone else that was foisted upon you?

The Mind of Christ Is the Cross

89

MARK 15:27–32 ESV | And with him they crucified two robbers, one on his right and one on his left. And those who passed by derided him, wagging their heads and saying, "Aha! You who would destroy the temple and rebuild it in three days, save yourself, and come down from the cross!" So also the chief priests with the scribes mocked him to one another, saying, "He saved others; he cannot save himself. Let the Christ, the King of Israel, come down now from the cross that we may see and believe." Those who were crucified with him also reviled him.

Consider This

Complete and utter forsakenness. Betrayed by Judas. Denied by Peter. Abandoned by the Twelve. Convicted by the Sanhedrin. Condemned by Pilate. Crucified by soldiers. Insulted by passersby. Mocked by the chief priests and the teachers of the Law. Insulted by his companions on crosses.

Tomorrow it will be, "My God. My God, why have you forsaken me?"

Never before and never since has something so bad happened to someone so good.

So why did we hate him so much? What did he do to deserve such vitriol?

In the end, he was left absolutely alone.

Whatever it is that you are going through right now, no matter how warranted or undeserved it may be, he understands.

During the days of Jesus' life on earth, he offered up prayers and petitions with fervent cries and tears to the one who could save him from death, and he was heard because of his reverent submission. Son though he was, he learned obedience from what he suffered and, once made perfect, he became the source of eternal salvation for all who obey him (see Hebrews 5:7–9).

In Paul's letter to the church at Phillipi he exhorted the believers to

> have the same mindset as Christ Jesus: Who, being in very nature God, did not consider equality with God something to be used to his own advantage; rather, he made himself nothing by taking the very nature of a servant, being made in human likeness. And being found in appearance as a man, he humbled himself by becoming obedient to death—even death on a cross! (Phil. 2:5–8)

When we consider the suffering of Jesus in his crucifixion, we immediately think about it through the lens of him doing this for us, and this is true. Paul seems to be taking a lot further than that. He is asking us to have the same mind in us. Clearly, we cannot do what Jesus did in a way that would redeem others, but we can do what Jesus did in ways that extend his redemptive work to others.

How would we do this? It will not start with our actions, but with our mentality. We can begin to grasp the mind of Christ simply by watching him and observing the grace with which endured all he endured.

What might that mean for us to endure the trials and tribulations we face with the mentality of the mind of Christ? What might it look like to humble ourselves? And, to be clear, being humbled doesn't always translate into humility. Humility is an obedient response to hardship. What might it look like to lay aside our mentality of, "Why is this happening to me?" in order to take up the mind of Christ, who endured all things with a patient trust in the ultimate outcome.

And let's not forget the rest of the story,

> Therefore God exalted him to the highest place and gave him the name that is above every name, that at the name of Jesus every knee should bow, in heaven and on earth and under the earth, and every tongue acknowledge that Jesus Christ is Lord, to the glory of God the Father. (Phil. 2:9–11)

From complete and utter forsakenness to complete and utter glory. The mind of Christ is the cross.

Think about a present trial or hardship you are going through, a cross you are bearing. Would it change your approach to this difficult season to know that the mentality with which you handle it could reveal something of the nature and love of God to someone who is paying attention?

The Prayer

Spirit of the living God, fall afresh on me.

The Questions

- What might it mean for you to have the same mind in you that was in Christ Jesus in the midst of this suffering?

90 When You Find Yourself in the Deepest Darkness

MARK 15:33–37 NRSV | When it was noon, darkness came over the whole land until three in the afternoon. At three o'clock Jesus cried out with a loud voice, "Eloi, Eloi, lema sabachthani?" which means, "My God, my God, why have you forsaken me?" When some of the bystanders heard it, they said, "Listen, he is calling for Elijah." And someone ran, filled a sponge with sour wine, put it on a stick, and gave it to him to drink, saying, "Wait, let us see whether Elijah will come to take him down." Then Jesus gave a loud cry and breathed his last.

Consider This

Sometimes we need to get up to a higher altitude and look at the bigger picture unfolding in Scripture. Today is one of those days. Today's text opens with these words.

When it was noon, darkness came over the whole land until three in the afternoon. This is a divinely inspired echo of the account of the creation of the world, "In the beginning God created the heavens and the earth. Now the earth was formless and empty, darkness was over the surface of the deep, and the Spirit of God was hovering over the waters" (Gen. 1:1–2).

Remember the next words from the mouth of God? Yep. "Let there be light!" The darkness described in today's text is the darkness of chaos preceding the death and resurrection of the Light of the World.

It gets better. Today's text also echoes the defining event in the life of the Hebrew people: the exodus. Remember those ten plagues? I want us to remember plague #9 in particular. Here's an account.

> Then the LORD said to Moses, "Stretch out your hand toward the sky so that darkness spreads over Egypt—darkness that can be felt." So Moses stretched out his hand toward the sky, and total darkness covered all Egypt for three days. No one could see anyone else or move about for three days. Yet all the Israelites had light in the places where they lived. (Exod. 10:21–23)

Now, recall plague #10: the death of all the firstborn sons of Egypt. It was the blood of the Passover lambs that saved the people of God from this unthinkable loss.

Then Jesus gave a loud cry and breathed his last.

Talk about "darkness that can be felt." The firstborn and only Son of God, the Lamb of God, who takes away the sins of the world, who brought deliverance from sin and death for all who will believe. As the old hymn puts it, "Nothing but the blood of Jesus."

Behold this incredible tapestry of salvation. The cross stands as the divine turning point from darkness to light and from death to life.

Sometimes we need to get up to a higher altitude and look at the bigger picture unfolding in Scripture. Do you see why today is one of those days?

And the practical application on a day like today? Awe. "Thank you for the cross!" We should point out in the midst of all of this cosmic drama we hear Jesus cry out these words:

At three o'clock Jesus cried out with a loud voice, "Eloi, Eloi, lema sabachthani?" which means, "My God, my God, why have you forsaken me?"

It turns out he wasn't forsaken after all. So the next time you are feeling forsaken by God, get to a higher place of perspective and remember the bigger story. It's in the lowest of low places that the greatest miracles often happen.

Now back to awe!

The Prayer

Spirit of the living God, fall afresh on me.

The Questions

- Have you ever found yourself in a place of darkness or forsakenness only to be met with God's presence and power on the other side of it? Consider sharing with your group.

Why We Say "Thank God It's Friday"

91

MARK 15:38–41 | The curtain of the temple was torn in two from top to bottom. And when the centurion, who stood there in front of Jesus, saw how he died, he said, "Surely this man was the Son of God!"

Some women were watching from a distance. Among them were Mary Magdalene, Mary the mother of James the younger and of Joseph, and Salome. In Galilee these women had followed him and cared for his needs. Many other women who had come up with him to Jerusalem were also there.

Consider This

It is hard to overestimate the magnitude of what happened on this particular Friday in world history.

Up to this point, the temple had been the central focus of the people of God; the location of the presence of God on earth. Everything revolved around this center. The place served as both symbol and sign. For over a thousand years the sins of the people of God were atoned for by the blood sacrifice of animals in the temple of God.

On this particular Friday in world history there would be a catastrophic change.

The curtain of the temple was torn in two from top to bottom.

That the ripping came from top to bottom indicated no human being had done it. On a nearby hill outside the city, another sacrifice unfolded. Something cosmic and eternal was happening. I want you to read this passage from Hebrews very carefully.

> But when Christ came as high priest of the good things that are now already here, he went through the greater and more perfect tabernacle that is not made with human hands, that is to say, is not a part of this creation. He did not enter by means of the blood of goats and calves; but he entered the Most Holy Place once for all by his own blood, thus obtaining eternal redemption. The blood of goats and bulls and the ashes of a heifer sprinkled on those who are ceremonially unclean sanctify them so that they are outwardly clean. How much more, then, will the blood of Christ, who through the eternal Spirit offered himself unblemished to God, cleanse our consciences from acts that lead to death, so that we may serve the living God! (Heb. 9:11–14)

The symbol of the temple was being replaced with the sign of the cross. A most feared sign of unadulterated terror and death took the place of the most cherished symbol of the presence of God. Even more, this most feared sign of unfathomable cruelty and insufferable pain would become the most hallowed sign on earth. How on earth could this be possible? Because nothing is impossible with God. In fact, this is the message of the cross. Absolutely nothing is beyond the redemption of Jesus. Now read this additional text from Hebrews carefully.

Therefore, brothers and sisters, since we have confidence to enter the Most Holy Place by the blood of Jesus, by a new and living way opened for us through the curtain, that is, his body, and since we have a great priest over the house of God, let us draw near to God with a sincere heart and with the full assurance that faith brings, having our hearts sprinkled to cleanse us from a guilty conscience and having our bodies washed with pure water. Let us hold unswervingly to the hope we profess, for he who promised is faithful. (Heb. 10:19–23)

His body is the new curtain. His blood is the new and living way. His priesthood is forever established. He doesn't give us a set of rules and regulations by which to approach God. He is the way himself! It's why before we were called Christians they called us, "People of the Way." This way is alive and open and beckons us to draw near!

There's more. You and I, as the followers of Jesus, are more than followers. We are ambassadors and priests. I think of us as the low priests in contrast with Jesus, the high priest. Our commission is to be filled with his Spirit that we might represent his presence in the world—especially to the low places. Nothing, absolutely nothing, is beyond the scope and scale of his redemption.

And when the centurion, who stood there in front of Jesus, saw how he died, he said, "Surely this man was the Son of God!"

And the fact that a Roman centurion, one of the executioners of Jesus, was the first to truly get it—takes it over the top. Confidence! Assurance! Hope! Wow! And all of this on a Friday. That's why we say thank God it's Friday!

Though we can draw near any day at any time, what if Fridays could become a focused "Drawing Near Day." Just thinking aloud. (That's the way Methodists think, I guess.) Pray for this assurance. It is a gift of the Holy Spirit. He wants us to ask for it. It's part of the process. This is real. The only thing holding us back is us.

The Prayer

Spirit of the living God, fall afresh on me.

The Questions

- What would it look like for confidence, assurance, and hope to rise up within you?
- What keeps you from drawing near to God?

92 Tired of Following Jesus in Secret?

MARK 15:42–47 ESV | And when evening had come, since it was the day of Preparation, that is, the day before the Sabbath, Joseph of Arimathea, a respected member of the council, who was also himself looking for the kingdom of God, took courage and went to Pilate and asked for the body of Jesus. Pilate was surprised to hear that he should have already died.

And summoning the centurion, he asked him whether he was already dead. And when he learned from the centurion that he was dead, he granted the corpse to Joseph. And Joseph bought a linen shroud, and taking him down, wrapped him in the linen shroud and laid him in a tomb that had been cut out of the rock. And he rolled a stone against the entrance of the tomb. Mary Magdalene and Mary the mother of Joses saw where he was laid.

Consider This

He asked for the body of Jesus.

He was an ordinary Joe. You know the type: good citizen, tither, respected member of the council, a leader people looked up to. If Joseph of Arimathea was on board, you could trust the deal was legit.

He had a solid reputation as an upstanding citizen. Why on earth was he stepping out of the crowd now, approaching the governor and asking for the body of this crucified peasant?

Joseph had no idea Jesus would be raised from the dead. No one did. Joseph, we are told, *was also himself waiting for the kingdom of God.* In John's gospel, we get this little bit of information:

> Now Joseph was a disciple of Jesus, but secretly because he feared the Jewish leaders. With Pilate's permission, he came and took the body away. He was accompanied by Nicodemus, the man who earlier had visited Jesus at night. (John 19:38–39)

Joseph and Nicodemus were secret disciples of Jesus. Why did they keep it secret? They were filled with the fear of their peers. If ever there were a moment to walk away and admit he had been wrong, it would have been this one. The secret would have never been known. He and Nicodemus could have gone back to life as they knew it.

Something must have clicked with Joseph. He probably watched in horror as his colleagues mercilessly heaped shame and scorn on this man he secretly followed. Something rose up in him and said, "Enough!" I bet he wished he had stood up to them long before. He knew what he had to do now. There's a little word in the text today that signals a departure from business as usual for Joseph of Arimathea. Did you catch it? The word is "boldly."

Joseph, we are told in the NIV, *"went boldly to Pilate and asked for Jesus' body."*

Joseph finally went public with his faith, when he probably thought it was way past too late. Imagine his exuberant delight when he discovered he had been right on time.

My hunch is there are thousands upon thousands of Joseph of Arimatheas among us. They believe, but they keep it secret. Why? Mostly, they fear what other people will think; that they will be labeled some kind of religious fanatic or an unapproachable "holier than thou" type or one who wears their religion on their sleeve. It's just easier to wear two hats; one with the Christian friends and another one with everybody else.

I remember being that guy. I considered myself a believer, but I'm not sure you would have had any idea of it. Looking back, I don't consider that I was a hypocrite. It's just that I lived in different compartments depending on which world I happened to be in. Somewhere along the way, I stepped out of that secret life and I went boldly. I've never looked back.

It's always kind of fun to see secret followers of Jesus happen to find one another out. It usually takes whatever level of relationship they had before to the tenth power. Imagine what it was like when Joseph and Nicodemus found each other out. It's awe-inspiring to see these two secret disciples finally come out into the light as the sun set on that Good Friday.

The Prayer
Spirit of the living God, fall afresh on me.

The Questions
- Is it time for you to go public? What might boldness look like for you today?

Why Faith Has to Die 93

MARK 16:1–3 NRSV | When the sabbath was over, Mary Magdalene, and Mary the mother of James, and Salome bought spices, so that they might go and anoint him. And very early on the first day of the week, when the sun had risen, they went to the tomb. They had been saying to one another, "Who will roll away the stone for us from the entrance to the tomb?"

Consider This

"Who will roll away the stone for us from the entrance to the tomb?"

What a question! Let that roll around in your mind a little bit and then off your tongue. Speak it aloud so your ears can hear yourself ask it.

"Who will roll away the stone for us from the entrance to the tomb?"

Given our vantage point in history and hindsight, it is next to impossible for us to imagine just how unimaginably unexpected the resurrection of Jesus would have been to these three women.

These women were tired and grief-stricken and yet they were doing what women do—which is the next good thing. Don't you ever wonder where Peter, James, and John were and why they weren't there with the women that morning? I suppose if they had been there, the women wouldn't have been asking this question.

"Who will roll away the stone for us from the entrance to the tomb?"

This is the essential question. It's a most practical question. At the same time, it holds profound theological meaning. They knew somehow they would figure it out, they just didn't yet know how. That's kind of how faith works. We know and we don't know. We don't know who will roll the stone away from the entrance of the tomb. We know we can't do it. But we go anyway. Pardon the cheap rhyme, but I can't resist. Faith means going without knowing. I mean, they knew it had to be done and they knew what they had to do, and they didn't have it all figured out, but they got up early and they went to the tomb.

This is how faith works. Here's what hits me the hardest about this text. Yesterday afternoon, the faith of these women had been utterly crushed. The ashes of their hopes were already cold. This story had ended badly, worse than anyone could have ever conceived of. They didn't have any faith left, and yet they did. It was the faith to get up early and do the next good thing that had to be done. It was not the supernatural faith that Jesus would be raised from the dead. It was the humble faith of love that goes to the tomb to anoint the dead body.

This is where God meets us. He meets us on the day after our faith dies (or whatever we conceived of as our faith before). As we are on our way to the tomb to do what has to be done—because life goes on—having no idea of "who will roll away the stone." That's where it happens. This is the place where the first light of resurrection dawns. It happens in a place of death, unexpectedly and unannounced, and it upends everything we thought faith was before. It exposes that our faith was actually only faith in what we hoped would happen and how we most wanted things to turn out. This is the beginning—or perhaps the deep renewal—of faith in God, in the resurrection of Jesus, in the open ended and limitless possibilities of the kingdom of God now unfolding before your very eyes.

Not how you thought it would happen—yet immeasurably above and beyond all you could ever ask or think.

"Who will roll away the stone for us from the entrance to the tomb?"

The Prayer

Spirit of the living God, fall afresh on me.

The Questions

- How closely is your faith tied to your hoped-for outcomes in life? What if those outcomes are actually in the way of your faith?

94 Without the Resurrection, We've Got Nothing

MARK 16:4–8 | But when they looked up, they saw that the stone, which was very large, had been rolled away. As they entered the tomb, they saw a young man dressed in a white robe sitting on the right side, and they were alarmed.

"Don't be alarmed," he said. "You are looking for Jesus the Nazarene, who was crucified. He has risen! He is not here. See the place where they laid him. But go, tell his disciples and Peter, 'He is going ahead of you into Galilee. There you will see him, just as he told you.'"

Trembling and bewildered, the women went out and fled from the tomb. They said nothing to anyone, because they were afraid.

Consider This

Though the story of Jesus be anchored in human history, were Jesus not raised from the dead we would probably have no idea he ever existed. Chances are he would not have even made the history books. Though his teachings resonated depths of truth unheard before by human ears and though he performed astonishing miraculous signs and though he died a cruel, unjust death at the hands of Jewish leaders and Roman authorities, the story of Jesus would be just that—another story among the now millions of stories in the annals of history. The historical account of Jesus' life and death is now known to us only because of the gospel, or the good news, of his resurrection from the dead. Why would Jesus matter more than any other historical figure who said and did amazing things?

This cannot be overstated. Paul said it emphatically in his letter to the church at Corinth, "And if Christ has not been raised, our preaching is useless and so is your faith" (1 Cor. 15:14).

The resurrection of Jesus is the upending of death, which is the curse of sin, which is eternal alienation of the creature from the Creator, which is the fundamental inescapable problem of the human race.

> For since death came through a man, the resurrection of the dead comes also through a man. For as in Adam all die, so in Christ all will be made alive. But each in turn: Christ, the firstfruits; then, when he comes, those who belong to him. (1 Cor. 15:21–23)

Jesus' life, his words, deeds, miracles, signs, suffering, and death are all known to us because he is raised from the dead. This is why he is the way and the truth and the life and the exclusive Savior of the human race and the entire creation and the Lord of heaven and earth. No one else before or since rose from the dead. Sure, history is littered with true stories of miraculous resuscitations, but there are no resurrections from the dead, save one. Everyone who has ever lived has died and in one form or another has been buried. Only one has died, been buried, and on the third day raised from the dead.

If you had cancer and a doctor told you there was only one known cure for your form of cancer, what would you do? Would you want to debate the injustice of this exclusive claim? No! You would thank God the terminal nature of your life could be extended beyond the terminal nature of your cancer. You would ask the doctor to treat you with the cure. So why is it that people bristle at the statement that Jesus

Christ is the only known cure to the cancer of sin and the curse of death? He is not withholding this cure (i.e., salvation) from anyone but offering it freely to all who will receive it. What news could be better than this? Because of his resurrection from the dead, not only do we know Jesus can cure the cancer of sin, we know he has actually reversed its consequences (i.e., death). In all of the history of the world and in all of eternity to come, nothing is more astonishing than this. This, my friends, is why men and women have given their lives to go to the ends of the earth for more than two thousand years now to share this gospel with anyone who will hear and receive it.

Without the resurrection, all we've got is at best another self-help strategy—Tony Robbins on steroids. With the resurrection, we have the whole gospel. Without the resurrection, if we even happen to discover Jesus in the stacks of history's library, we may at best find some help so we can try harder to become better people. With the resurrection, comes the power of the Holy Spirit to not only cleanse us from guilt and heal us from shame, but to supernaturally empower us to overcome sin, which has lost its power. Without the resurrection, we would still have the Old Testament of the Bible but we wouldn't have any real access to it. We wouldn't understand it as our story, because after all, we are (most of us) Gentiles. Our T-shirts might say something like, "We came. We saw. We died." With the resurrection, we have the whole council of God and the sure hope of our own resurrection because we have given our lives to the Risen One. And far more than a T-shirt slogan, we have the proclamation which goes like this: He is risen!

The Prayer

Spirit of the living God, fall afresh on me.

The Questions

- Where does this challenge your faith today? Where do you feel pushback?

95 | What Faith Is and What It Is Not

MARK 16:9–13 | When Jesus rose early on the first day of the week, he appeared first to Mary Magdalene, out of whom he had driven seven demons. She went and told those who had been with him and who were mourning and weeping. When they heard that Jesus was alive and that she had seen him, they did not believe it.

Afterward Jesus appeared in a different form to two of them while they were walking in the country. These returned and reported it to the rest; but they did not believe them either.

Consider This

No one making up a story in the first century in the ancient Near East would have ever listed women as the eyewitnesses of the empty tomb. According to Jewish law, a women's eyewitness testimony was not admissible as legitimate evidence. This would have been a very inconvenient truth. The fact of its inclusion in the Gospel of Mark creates a quite ironic reverse effect. That the eyewitness account came from women actually increases its credibility because the fact of its inclusion in the story corroborates its authenticity. In other words, as I began, no one making up a story in the first century in the ancient Near East would have ever listed women as the eyewitnesses of the empty tomb—if they wanted anyone to believe them.

The most interesting aspect of today's text is the way the disciples chose not to believe the eyewitness accounts of Jesus' resurrection. Why didn't they believe? Of all people, wouldn't these dejected disciples have wanted to believe it the most? They did not believe. They had no faith. Why not? They had eyewitness testimony from credible witnesses they trusted.

Here's why I think they didn't believe. It's the same reason people do not believe to this very day. Despite the fact of real and trustworthy evidence, I don't think faith in the resurrection of Jesus Christ can be built on this kind of foundation. Nor can faith be built on internal subjective feelings, though I believe faith involves feelings.

Faith cannot be built on evidence that can be seen, added up, or somehow proven. As we see in the opening words of the eleventh chapter of Hebrews, "Faith is the substance of things hoped for, the evidence of things not seen." Faith is of another order entirely. Faith is the fruit of divine revelation. Do you remember when Peter made his famous confession of Jesus? "You are the Messiah, the Son of the living God." Do you remember what Jesus said to him? "Blessed are you, Simon son of Jonah, for this was not revealed to you by flesh and blood, but by my Father in heaven" (Matt. 16:16–17).

Are you tracking with me? This is a nuanced thing I'm trying to communicate which could be easily misunderstood. I believe the bodily resurrection of Jesus Christ is a fact of history. I also believe billions of people throughout history have enjoyed an internal subjective experience of the resurrection. Faith, however, is neither a fruit of historical evidence nor of the testimony of another's subjective experience. Faith is the fruit of divine revelation wherein the Holy Spirit works in the human heart to convince one of a reality that could not otherwise be whole heartedly embraced.

"If you confess with your mouth that Jesus is Lord and believe in your heart that God raised him from the dead then you will be saved" (Rom. 10:9).

The Prayer

Spirit of the living God, fall afresh on me.

The Questions

- How do you assess your own faith in the resurrection of Jesus Christ? Is it a static, flat kind of belief or is it a growing, dynamic, living reality?

The Wisdom behind a Good, Old-Fashioned Trust Fall

96

MARK 16:14–18 ESV | Afterward he appeared to the eleven themselves as they were reclining at table, and he rebuked them for their unbelief and hardness of heart, because they had not believed those who saw him after he had risen. And he said to them, "Go into all the world and proclaim the gospel to the whole creation. Whoever believes and is baptized will be saved, but whoever does not believe will be condemned. And these signs will accompany those who believe: in my name they will cast out demons; they will speak in new tongues; they will pick up serpents with their hands; and if they drink any deadly poison, it will not hurt them; they will lay their hands on the sick, and they will recover."

Consider This

Did you catch the reason Jesus rebuked his disciples?

and he rebuked them for their unbelief and hardness of heart, because they had not believed those who saw him after he had risen.

This brings us back to the previous conversation about the nature of faith—what it is and what it is not.

Faith is the fruit of divine revelation wherein the Holy Spirit works in the human heart to convince one of a reality that could not otherwise be wholeheartedly embraced.

One of the big problems with the way we think about faith is how we have allowed it to be framed by intellectual and scientific categories. It needs to make sense to our rational selves. We need to see some sort of scientific evidence beyond a reasonable doubt in order to consider it trustworthy to believe. Faith is on another plane. It operates in the real world yet from another dimension. Faith lives in the realm of divine revelation.

To better ascertain how we think about faith we need only define what we see as its opposite. Typically, people think the opposite of faith is doubt. In reality, doubt lives very close to faith. In fact, doubt may be a necessary precondition for faith. Let's consider this through the proverbial lens of a trust fall. You know what I'm talking about—when a group cajoles one of their friends to stand up on a table and fall backward into the secure net of our linked-up arms below. As the person stands on the table, he or she is already walking in the realm of faith. Doubt is simply part of the equation. I'm really not doubting if they will catch me. I'm doubting whether I have the courage to actually relinquish my control over myself. And why am I doubting this? It's because of my fear. Fear, not doubt, is the opposite of faith. Think of a continuum with fear on the far left end and faith on the far right end.

Fear is the default condition of the human race. It's why the first words from any messenger from God in the Bible are, "Do not be afraid." This is doubly the case with Jesus. Left alone, our fear inevitably leads us to profound levels of self-protection and a deep need to be in control. Faith is the movement from self-preservation to self-abandonment, from self-protection to God's protection, and from my need to be in control to a surrendering to the control of God.

Faith is the movement from fear through doubt into courage and onward to faith, which is an active trust in the promise of God's goodness. If I'm standing on the table, I have already confronted my fear and now face the battle between doubt and courage. Falling backward is the act of abandoning myself into the secure arms of someone other than myself.

Do you see how doubt is not the failure to trust God but the beginning of moving beyond trusting in oneself. Doubt is a step in the right direction.

Jesus is not worried about our doubt. He is concerned with how fear so easily leads to taking steps in the wrong direction. So if doubt is a step in the right direction, what is a step in the wrong direction? It's the "stubborn refusal to believe." The stubborn refusal to believe has little to do with eyewitnesses or evidence or scientific proofs and everything to do with our broken ability to trust. I think the disciples found themselves espousing the commonly held human mentality of, "Fool me once, shame on you. Fool me twice, shame on me." They had bet the farm on the wrong horse. There was no way in you-know-where they were about to believe Jesus was raised from the dead.

The stubborn refusal to believe is a doubling down of taking back control. My own need to be in complete control of my own life makes me my own god, which takes us all the way back to the garden of Eden and what went wrong in the first place. It's why the garden of Gethsemane is so critical for us as a matter of our own discipleship (i.e., "Not my will but your will be done").

So where do you find yourself on the continuum: Stubborn Refusal to Believe—Fear—Doubt—Courage—Faith—Abandoned to God? How does this way of thinking help you to approach those who stubbornly refuse to believe? Remember, Jesus rebuked his disciples, but many people who live in this place of refusal have never gotten anywhere near discipleship. Might we want to have compassion for the kind of brokenness that may lie beneath that refusal.

The Prayer

Spirit of the living God, fall afresh on me.

The Questions

- What is it that you are afraid of when it comes to trusting God?
- What situations create a need in you to be in control?

How the Gospels Disciple Us in the Gospel

97

MARK 16:19–20 | After the Lord Jesus had spoken to them, he was taken up into heaven and he sat at the right hand of God. Then the disciples went out and preached everywhere, and the Lord worked with them and confirmed his word by the signs that accompanied it.

Consider This

And so we come to the end of our Gospel of Mark journey.

I've read Mark a lot of times over the years, and every time I find Jesus disciples me even more in the ways of the kingdom.

One of the interesting things about all the Gospels is the way they end with a new beginning. Even more interesting is the way this new beginning is actually an invitation to go back to the beginning of the gospel itself. The gospel doesn't launch us out with a "Been there. Done that. Got the T-Shirt" mentality. We don't somehow graduate from the gospel and head out on our own to do whatever seems best to us beyond that. We go forward to live into and out of the Gospels of Matthew, Mark, Luke, and John. They are the ongoing life-long curriculum for our own discipleship. At the same time, they serve as training for mission and evangelism and provide a textbook for discipling others in the Way.

It makes sense, doesn't it? The Gospels give us detailed and theologically loaded accounts of how Jesus discipled his disciples. We can be sure these documents continually guided the disciples in discipling the next generation of believers and so on and so on.

What if that's the big problem with discipleship today, that we have gotten away from the Gospels as the core discipleship curriculum for the New Testament church. Sure, we draw from them, but in the process we import the content into our own frameworks and to serve our own agendas. As biblical as those agendas may be, I'd say it's impossible to be more biblical than the Bible itself. In other words, we can put all sorts of biblical stuff together to make disciples, but what if the Holy Spirit has put it together just like Jesus wants it in the Gospels themselves? What if the point is not only their content but their framework, format, and flow? What if biblical discipleship means the Gospels themselves are our curriculum rather than extracting biblical principles from them for discipleship? Do you see the difference?

Then the disciples went out and preached everywhere, and the Lord worked with them and confirmed his word by the signs that accompanied it.

What if we don't so much see the signs that accompany the gospel these days because we've gotten off track in the way we make disciples?

The Prayer
Spirit of the living God, fall afresh on me.

The Questions

- What would it mean to disciple people not only with the content of the gospel message, but with the context of the Gospels and the way they unfold?

2011-

Transformational

CPSIA information can be obtained
at www.ICGtesting.com
Printed in the USA
LVHW040714230819
628513LV00004B/4/P